HISTORY OF 99 SQUADRON

INDEPENDENT FORCE
ROYAL AIR FORCE
MARCH, 1918—NOVEMBER, 1918

BY
SQUADRON-LEADER L. A. PATTINSON
D.S.O., M.C., D.F.C.

The Naval & Military Press Ltd
in association with
The Imperial War Museum
Department of Printed Books

Published jointly by
The Naval & Military Press Ltd
Unit 10 Ridgewood Industrial Park,
Uckfield, East Sussex,
TN22 5QE England
Tel: +44 (0) 1825 749494
Fax: +44 (0) 1825 765701
www.naval-military-press.com

and

The Imperial War Museum, London
Department of Printed Books
www.iwm.org.uk

In reprinting in facsimile from the original, any imperfections are inevitably reproduced and the quality may fall short of modern type and cartographic standards.

DE HAVILAND 9.

HISTORY OF
99 SQUADRON
INDEPENDENT FORCE
ROYAL AIR FORCE
MARCH, 1918—NOVEMBER, 1918

BY

SQUADRON-LEADER L. A. PATTINSON
D.S.O., M.C., D.F.C.

CAMBRIDGE:
W. HEFFER & SONS Ltd.
1920

Foreword

In writing this book, the Author has considered himself the servant of the Squadron's past and present members.

Only such facts have been recorded as were thought to bear directly on the Unit's ability to carry out its work. Sentiment and artificial literary effect have been carefully ignored, and a serious attempt has been made to prevent the author's personal opinions from appearing.

The accounts of operations are based on a diary and other information available on November 11th, 1918; and no attempt has been made to include information subsequently acquired.

The story opens at the date on which mobilisation definitely commenced with the appointment of a Commanding Officer, whose duty was solely in connection with active service.

November 11th, 1918, is the date at which such a history naturally ends.

It is hoped that the note on formation flying and the technical detail with regard to engine failure, petrol consumption, failure of individual machines, workshop organisation, etc., will throw a light on the details of a squadron's work necessarily absent in a general history of the Royal Air Force.

The Author gratefully acknowledges the assistance of Squadron-Leader C. R. Cox, A.F.C., and Flight Lieutenant W. D. Thom, D.F.C., in supplying an account of the operations in October and November, and of Major H. W. M. Paul, O.B.E., M.C., in providing much useful information, collected by him as Intelligence Officer of the Independent Force.

The Air Ministry accepts no responsibility for the accuracy of statements contained in this volume.

List of Photographs Illustrating the History of 99 Squadron

Frontispiece .. A DE HAVILAND 9

REGISTERED NO.			DATE.	SUBJECT.
99 D.A. No.		7	21/5/18	Bombs bursting on Railway Triangle at Metz Sablon.
,,	,,	14	27/5/18	Bombs bursting near Bensdorf sidings.
,,	,,	50	13/6/18	Dillingen Factory and Station, with bombs bursting on and near the Station.
,,	,,	60	25/6/18	Bursts on the Railway sidings at Offenburg.
,,	,,	66	30/6/18	Hagenau Aerodrome, with bombs bursting clear of the hangars.
,,	,,	69	8/7/18	Buhl Aerodrome, showing bomb burst on or beside the largest shed.
,,	,,	77	16/7/18	Destruction of Thionville Goods Station. (1) Direct hit on an ammunition train.
,	,,	80	16/7/18	Destruction of Thionville Goods Station. (2) The smoke spreading.
,,	,,	83	17/7/18	Bursts alongside the river at Thionville and damage done on 16th.
				German photographs of destruction of Thionville Goods Station : (1) Sidings with remains of ammunition train. (2) General view of main lines and rolling stock. (3) Site of two very large warehouses.
,,	,,	93	22/7/18	Offenburg, with bombs bursting on Station and sidings.
,,	,,	94	do.	Offenburg, with bombs bursting on Station and sidings a few seconds later.
,,	,,	115	2/9/18	Buhl Aerodrome, with two hangars enveloped in smoke.
,,	,,	116	do.	The same, showing, in addition, a direct hit on a hangar.
55 D.A.	,,	2100	2/9/18	Photograph by 55 Squadron, showing more bursts on Buhl Aerodrome.
99 D.A.	,,	117} 118}	3/9/18	Bombs bursting on Morhange Aerodrome.
104 D.A.	,,	63	4/9/18	Bursts on Morhange Aerodrome.
99 D.A.	,,	121	do.	More bursts on Morhange Aerodrome.
,,	,,	148	14/9/18	Railway Triangle at Metz Station, with smoke from bombs.
,,	,,	161	16/9/18	Bombs bursting on Hagenau Aerodrome.

Photograph of D.H. 9A machine giving general view.

History of 99 Squadron

On March 11th, command of this Squadron was taken over by Major L. A. Pattinson, M.C., from Capt. A. M. Swyny.

There were still a considerable number of pupils under training on D.H. 6's, B.E. 2 E's, 160 Beardmore A.W.'s and D.H. 9's, of which machines a large proportion were unserviceable owing to the lack of experience of the fitters, and also to the fact that the main planes of the D.H. 9's were mostly of an unmodified type, which had to be changed. The Squadron was in a generally unsettled condition, as there were no Flight Commanders on the strength, who were due to proceed with it overseas.

On March 16th, orders were received that training was to cease and training machines to be sent away. The Squadron was quickly reduced to some twenty-four pilots, from whom were to be selected those for overseas. Of these pilots a few had still some final tests to pass before joining the majority, who, as pupils, were still on finishing courses at Marske-on-Sea and Stonehenge. Little flying was accomplished between this date and the procedure of the Squadron overseas, except tests and practice in map-reading for the journey to France. This was due to the fact of many officers and other ranks being away on leave; the fitters being very inexperienced, and particularly so on the B.H.P. engine; and many machines being unserviceable owing to the change of unmodified for modified planes, and the fitting of bomb-sights, Lewis gun drum-racks, Aldis sights, etc.

The period of mobilisation was one of great activity; the training of fitters to work on the 230 Siddeley Puma engine, and the arrangement of Squadron workshops being the matters which required most energy.

A change of Chief Master Mechanics occurred, owing to the sickness of C.M.M. J. Lane, who was passed medically unfit to proceed with the Squadron overseas, and replaced by C.M.M. D. Martin, M.M., whose great experience, energy and ability played a most important part in preparing the Squadron for active service.

Partly owing to the fact that the Flight Commanders were posted to the Squadron so shortly before proceeding overseas, and also as a matter of policy, a great amount of centralisation was carried out ; all carpenters, coppersmiths, electricians, instrument repairers and sailmakers being concentrated in the "Headquarters" Flight under the Chief Master Mechanic, and detailed by him, under the direct supervision of the Squadron-Commander, for work as necessary in the other Flights. The overhauls of all aero engines, magnetos, Remy ignition fittings, and carburettors were undertaken by the Headquarters Flight, as was also all electrical work on hangars, charging and testing of accumulators on machines, and repairs to planes, except those of a very trivial character.

All fittings for machines were made to Squadron standard pattern and fitted under the supervision of the N.C.O.'s responsible for their manufacture. At the time when the machines were flown overseas, they were complete with fittings, and there were in addition six sets of these in reserve. The following Flight Commanders were posted to the Squadron for Overseas :

On April 9th, Capt. W. D. Thom, whose previous service had been with Corps Squadrons in France as a pilot.

On March 25th, Capt. P. C. Purser, M.C., whose experience in France was limited to that of an observer on fighting and reconnaissance work during the battle of the Somme.

On March 21st, Capt. A. D. Taylor, who had also served with the R.F.C. as an observer in France in a Bombing and Reconnaissance Squadron.

Of the pilots who were finally posted for service overseas, only one had ever been in action as a pilot, and only three had ever flown across the lines in any capacity. The Squadron was therefore prepared to receive gladly all the information that could possibly be obtained from other Bombing Squadrons, on arrival in France.

On April 17th, mobilisation was completed. At least 50 per cent. of personnel had arrived within a fortnight of that date, and this led to much confusion, especially as the Chief Mechanics and Sergeant Mechanics were mostly inexperienced, and the Flight Commanders had so recently joined.

PERSONNEL OF THE SQUADRON

The Officer personnel of the Squadron finally selected to proceed overseas was as follows :—

"HEADQUARTERS" FLIGHT.

Squadron-Commander	Major L. A. PATTINSON, M.C.
Recording Officer	Lieut. C. C. GARDNER.
Equipment Officer	2nd Lieut. R. W. ATCHLEY.
Armament Officer	Lieut. J. RIMMER.

"A" FLIGHT.

Pilots.	Observers.
Capt. W. D. THOM (*Commander*).	Lieut. C. G. CLAYE.
Lieut. E. L. DOIDGE.	2nd Lieut. W. B. WALKER.
Lieut. N. S. HARPER.	2nd Lieut. D. G. BENSON.
2nd Lieut. C. S. JOHNSON.	2nd Lieut. T. K. LUDGATE.
2nd Lieut. O. JONES.	2nd Lieut. E. BEALE.
2nd Lieut. K. D. MARSHALL.	2nd Lieut. O. BELL.
(*Spare*) 2nd Lieut. W. G. STEVENSON.	2nd Lieut. T. H. WIGGINS.

"B" FLIGHT.

Capt. P. C. PURSER, M.C. (*Commander*).	2nd Lieut. R. F. CONNELL.
Lieut. H. SANDERS.	2nd Lieut. W. W. A. JENKIN.
2nd Lieut. E. A. CHAPIN.	2nd Lieut. B. S. W. TAYLOR.
2nd Lieut. V. BEECROFT.	Lieut. N. T. MELVILLE.
2nd Lieut. W. J. GARRITY.	2nd Lieut. M. A. SKINNER.
2nd Lieut. S. M. BLACK.	2nd Lieut. E. SINGLETON.
(*Spare*) 2nd Lieut. J. W. RICHARDS.	2nd Lieut. E. J. MUNSON.

"C" FLIGHT.

Capt. A. D. TAYLOR (*Commander*).	Lieut. H. S. NOTLEY.
Lieut. D. A. MACDONALD.	2nd Lieut. F. H. BLAXILL.
2nd Lieut. C. C. CONOVER.	
2nd Lieut. M. T. S. PAPENFUS.	Lieut. A. L. BENJAMIN.
2nd Lieut. R. F. FREELAND.	2nd Lieut. R. E. SOTHCOTT.
2nd Lieut. H. D. WEST.	2nd Lieut. J. LEVY.
(*Spare*) 2nd Lieut. F. G. THOMPSON.	2nd Lieut. S. C. THORNLEY.

On April 18th, the transport, in charge of the Equipment Officer, proceeded to Portsmouth in time for embarkation on the 19th.

On the 20th, the personnel, with the exception of the fitters detailed to fly, left by rail in charge of Capt. Thom and the Recording Officer. The flying personnel then experienced a tiresome period of four days' inaction, with most depressing weather, alternating between very low clouds round Salisbury and fogs at Lympne.

On the 22nd, "B" and "C" Flights left the ground in formation, but were recalled owing to low clouds and bad visibility. Lieut. West took off with a bad swing, carrying away portions of the smoke-fire on his undercarriage, and causing considerable alarm to the group of distinguished spectators assembled to see the start. He lost touch with his formation, and finally arrived safely at Lympne.

On the afternoon of the 25th the weather improved considerably, but was still cloudy. All machines left, "A" Flight formation being led by the Squadron-Commander. A heavy thunderstorm was encountered about Dorking, and formations split up. The three rear machines of "A" Flight flew south to avoid the storm, and landed in very bad weather at Ford Junction Aerodrome, near Bognor; as did Lieut. Macdonald, of "C" Flight. All landed safely, with the exception of Lieut. Jones, whose machine was wrecked on a ridge at the edge of the aerodrome. Lieut. Freeland force-landed without accident at Telscombe. The remainder of the Squadron arrived at Lympne between 5.15 and 6.30 p.m. As the weather was reported from Marquise to be fit for crossing, seven pilots, who were able to get their machines ready, left between 7.15 and 7.30 with just sufficient time to reach St. Omer before dark. They found very thick mist on the French side. Lieut. Sanders, seeing that the weather was bad on the far coast, recrossed the Channel and landed in almost complete darkness at about 8.15 at Lympne. The remainder landed wherever they could see the ground through the mist. Of these six pilots, all landed without injury to themselves or their mechanics. Capts. Purser and Taylor, and Lieuts. Doidge and Conover flew to St. Omer on the 27th, having landed safely near Marquise. Lieut. Black crashed near Boulogne. Lieut. Harper landed successfully in the same area, started for St. Omer next day, and finally crashed on attempting a second forced landing in low clouds.

On the 26th and the morning of the 27th, the weather was unfit for crossing. The remainder of the pilots, who had arrived at Lympne on the 25th, crossed on the afternoon of the 27th, running into low clouds and rain on the French side. Major Pattinson and Lieuts. Sanders, Beecroft, Papenfus, and Jones arrived at St. Omer, but Lieuts. Garrity and Chapin lost themselves in the clouds and broke their machines on forced landings. Lieut. West, who left Lympne at the same time, landed at Marquise.

New machines were collected from Marquise to replace those crashed on the way; and in spite of bad weather, all had collected at St. Omer in serviceable condition by May 2nd.

On the next day the weather improved considerably, and the Squadron left in flight formations for Tantonville Aerodrome, south of Nancy. "A" and "B" Flights arrived safely with the exception of Lieut. Harper, who overshot the aerodrome and ran into a ditch, cutting his face badly and injuring Corpl. Harding severely, who was flying with him.

The start of "C" Flight was delayed by a leak, which developed in one of the radiators when the engines were being warmed up preparatory to starting. After flying for about thirty miles, Capt. Taylor's formation returned, owing to a severe thunderstorm.

Tantonville Aerodrome, which was shared with 55 Squadron, proved to be very inconvenient, as the other ranks were billeted in a village about two miles distant; there were inadequate cookhouses and workshops, and building was prohibited by the French authorities for fear of spoiling their excellent arrangements for camouflage. The long flight from St. Omer had disclosed the weaknesses of the B.H.P. engines, and broken valve springs and other small defects were found on nearly all. A very trying period commenced at this time, everybody being very busy learning the management of the engines, and fitting bomb-racks. The weather was, on the whole, very bad, and, being inexperienced, the Squadron took a considerable time to settle comfortable and to find out how to get the necessary work done.

Flying consisted largely of tests with and without dummy bombs, and occasional formation flying, which was much hindered by engine trouble. It was found that single machines could seldom climb above 16,000 feet in 75 minutes without bombs, or 14,000 feet in the same time with one 230 lb. or two 112 lb. bombs. Most engines ran very badly, and used far too much petrol above 10,000 feet, owing to the defective altitude control on the Zenith carburettor. This was afterwards enormously improved by a Squadron modification, and the average petrol consumption reduced from about 15 gallons an hour to less than 13.

The Squadron was indebted to 55 Squadron for many valuable hints about local landmarks, the nature of bombing operations in this area, and also for the type of six-machine formation, which was copied and proved to be very successful.

On May 8th and 9th bad weather stopped flying.

The bad weather continued over the 13th, on which day Lieuts. West and Freeland both attempted to come on from Compiegne, but lost their way in low clouds and broke their machines when making a forced landing south of Azelot. The two flights at Tantonville began to settle down and get rather better running from their engines.

Number of pilots flying 10
Total time flown .. .. 2 hrs. 50 min.
Number of flights for test or practice 10

On the next day 22 machines left the ground on practice and test flights. In all, 18 hours 45 minutes flying was done.

On May 15th, the remaining four machines of "C" Flight arrived safely from Paris in indifferent weather, after having flown there from Compiegne, so as to get their machines put in order.

"A" and "B" Flights produced their first six-machine formations. Capt. Thom's formation showed great promise, and all reached 15,000 feet, without bombs.

The same formation, with Major Pattinson flying as deputy-leader, did an excellent practice on the next day, flying very close together and keeping position well on turns. Although work in the air was still much impeded by engine trouble and the inexperience

Bombs Bursting on Railway Triangle at Metz-Sablon

MAY 19TH

of the fitters, formation flying improved very rapidly from this time onwards. A very good raid on Cologne by No. 55 Squadron cheered everybody considerably.

On the 19th, a record amount of practice flying was done, in spite of an enormous amount of engine trouble.

Number of pilots flying 18
Time flown test practice .. .. .. 37 hrs. 25 mins.
Number of flights for test or practice 26

Lieut. Johnson was admitted to Hospital, and did not rejoin the Squadron.

On the 20th, the Squadron performed its first official duties, six machines going on a line patrol in search of an enemy photographic machine, which, however, was not sighted.

On Tuesday, May 21st, the first bomb raid was carried out on Metz Sablon Railway Triangle with six machines, led by Capt. Thom. Eight machines left at 5.15 a.m., two being detailed as emergency machines. Two of the original formation dropped out before crossing the Lines: Lieut. Black with engine trouble, and Lieut. Chapin having lost position on a turn. The following pilots and observers finally completed the raid : Capt. Thom and Lieut. Claye, Lieuts. Marshall and Bell, Stevenson and Wiggins, Doidge and Walker, Beecroft and Melville, and Garrity and Skinner. The formation was very good, and excellent results were obtained. The observers reported ten bursts on the buildings and railway in the Triangle, one on the line just clear of the Triangle, and one in the town just west of the objective. A photograph taken on the raid confirms at least one burst in the centre of the Triangle, and three or four along the northern edge, of which one is a direct hit on the large warehouse, which appears to be on fire. (Photo. 99. D.A. 7 of 21/5/18.) These results were considered most satisfactory for inexperienced pilots over such a heavily defended area, and the Squadron was warmly congratulated by Brig.-Gen. C. L. N. Newall, A.M., the G.O.C. of the 8th Brigade, on its excellent beginning. Eighteen machines also left the ground on various practice flights.

On the next day the same target was again attacked at the same time by "A" Flight, and even better results obtained, all bombs being reported on some portion of the target. Photographs showed only a few bursts, but those were on the target. The six detailed machines all completed the duty, the emergency machines not being required. After these raids a very great deal of work was required, valve springs being broken on almost all the engines.

"B" and "C" Flights carried out a considerable amount of formation practice.

On the 23rd, the first raid with two formations of six machines each, was done on Metz Sablon by "B" and "C" Flights. They failed to meet as arranged, and the formations went separately. "B" Flight's formation went over with five machines and "C" Flight's with six. The observers reported 14 hits on the objective, and about eight of these were confirmed by photographs. The bombs were dropped from between 13,500 and 14,000 feet.

This day the Squadron lost Lieut. Conover, who was passed medically unfit for high flying.

The Squadron now had its first taste of fighting. Formations from "A" and "B" Flights, led by Capt. Thom and Lieut. Sanders respectively, started off to bomb Hagondange blast furnaces, about 25 miles over the Lines, in the Moselle Valley. "B" Flight formation completely failed to get together, and Lieuts. Sanders and Garrity joined in "A" Flight formation, which was under strength owing to engine trouble. Lieut. Beecroft's engine broke a connecting rod, and the pilot made a successful forced landing.

Just before reaching the objective the formation was attacked by seven or eight Albatros D 5 scouts, which stayed behind at about 200-300 yards. The formation closed excellently when attacked, and one E.A. was driven down out of control by the combined fire of Lieuts. Skinner and Walker, flying respectively with Lieuts. Garrity and Doidge. This machine dived vertically for about three or four thousand feet, and then spun down till lost to sight six or seven thousand feet below the formation. Lieuts. Jones and Skinner were both wounded in the leg, carrying on excellently after being hit. The majority of the bomb bursts were unobserved, but the leader reported that he saw a few which were wide of the target. There was a very strong wind, which, combined with the attack by

Bensdorf Sidings and Junction with Bombs Bursting.

E.A. before reaching the target and very heavy anti-aircraft fire, probably accounted for inaccurate bombing.

On Saturday, May 25th, the weather was, somewhat fortunately for the Squadron, unfit for service flying, and too bad for any but local tests. This was a very busy day, as several machines had been considerably damaged in the previous day's fight, and there was a great deal of work to be done on engines, including the top-overhauling of four and the changing of one.

The following pilots reported for duty :—Lieuts. J. H. Underwood, G. Broadbent and C. A. Vick.

The next day the weather was still unfit for operations, and the only flying done was on engine tests. A pair of carburettors, with altitude controls modified in the Squadron, were tried on D.H. 9 No. 6210, and gave excellent results, not only as regards altitude control, but in improved " opening out " when taking off. This pair of carburettors remained on Lieut. Stevenson's machine till it was finally wrecked, after having proved itself the best machine in the Squadron. On this day there were only six machines serviceable out of the fifteen on charge.

On the 27th, "B" and "C" Flights carried out a raid on Bensdorf Station, 16 miles over the Lines. The target was very narrow, but, on the whole, very good shooting was made. Observers claimed three bursts on the railway and several others very close. A photograph (99 D.A. 14) shows only four or five bursts, of which one has caused a fire in a building beside the railway, and three others are just north of the line. Considering that there was a very strong N.E. wind, and that the railway lies east and west, this was considered a very satisfactory raid. Of fourteen machines which left the ground, ten crossed the Lines. A few hostile machines were met, and unfortunately Lieuts. Macdonald and Blaxill fell out of the formation and were shot down. They landed safely with their machine disabled.

On the next day Bensdorf was again bombed. Eleven machines, out of the twelve detailed, completed the raid. These were from "A" and "B" Flights. There was an even stronger wind than on the previous day, and no direct hits were obtained, though the shooting was fairly accurate. A few hostile machines were seen and engaged indecisively at long range. Second Lieut. J. Whattam reported to the Squadron for duty as pilot.

The 29th was a thoroughly unlucky day. Fourteen machines of "A" and "C" Flights started for Thionville, 32 miles over the Lines. Finally, only six machines completed the raid. Of the eight which failed to cross the Lines, one machine broke a petrol pipe, another had a broken oil pipe, and a third a badly missing engine; the remainder were unable to keep up at a height owing principally to defective vacuum control and broken exhaust valve springs. There was a very strong wind and thick clouds, so Capt. Thom decided to bomb Metz Sablon. The bombs fell together on or about the Barracks, south-west of the Railway Triangle.

On the next day "B" and "C" Flights left at 4.45 a.m. for Thionville. Visibility was very bad, and Capt. Taylor brought his formation back without having crossed the Lines, being unable to find the other formation in the mist. Capt. Purser went to Metz with three other machines, the remainder having dropped out owing to engine trouble at a height. Fairly good bursts were reported on or near the railway, but the photographs taken of the objective were spoilt by mist. Two formations made a second attempt at 11.15 a.m. but found thick clouds over the Lines, and had to abandon the raid.

On the 31st, the bombing of Thionville was again attempted, the formation leaving at about 4.15 a.m. Ten machines reached the objective in very bad visibility and a very strong wind. No hits were reported on the target.

June 1st was a fine day, and an attempt was made by "A" and "B" Flights to start early for Metz, but owing to engine trouble the machines did not leave till 7.30 a.m. Eventually only six machines performed the raid out of the thirteen which started. The majority of the machines which did not cross the Lines were unable to keep pace at a height, and it was agreed, after talking the matter over, that leaders should attempt rather to take full formations over the Lines than to climb an extra 500 feet, which would in any case be insufficient to enable the D.H. 9's to avoid the German scouts. Owing to an indecisive combat with four of five enemy scouts, which

JUNE 2ND

attacked over the objective, the bursts were entirely unobserved. The wind was again about 25-30 miles per hour at 13,000 feet, and anti-aircraft fire was very heavy and accurate in the Moselle Valley. Lieut. Melville was slightly wounded in the head by a piece of shell-case, and was consequently away from duty for the following week. At this time the Squadron was passing through a period of depression. One or more valve springs had broken on at least three out of four engines which went up on a raid, and this, combined with frequent carburettor and petrol pipe troubles, made it most difficult for the fitters to keep the engines serviceable. The difficulties of the mechanics were largely augmented by their being billeted so far from the aerodrome. The pilots and observers were also much downcast by the frequent failure of the machines even to reach 13,000 feet in a reasonable time when carrying bombs.

On the 2nd, the wind was even stronger than on the previous day, and the weather rendered flying impossible till noon, after which there were large banks of cloud with fairly big gaps in places. "B" and "C" Flights left at 12.45 p.m., but failed to meet. The former bombed Metz Sablon with five machines, and the latter with six. "B" Flight's bombs were observed just clear of the line to the south of the Triangle, but the remainder were unobserved owing to clouds. The formations were very good, and the machines gave a more even performance.

The next day was devoted to work in the hangars and a practice formation flight for new pilots. A great deal of useful work was done on engines, and many small faults in fitting discovered and remedied. An expert from the Siddeley Company was attached for about ten days at this time, who helped considerably, but was unable to discover anything in connection with the maintenance of engines beyond what was already known to Chief Master Mechanic Martin. The first case of a cracked cylinder head was now found on an engine, and these became more frequent as the weather became warmer. A considerable improvement in Squadron organisation was made by concentrating all work on magnetos under one specially detailed instrument-repairer, and, passing all sparking plugs through a tester in Headquarters' workshops, cleaning and adjusting them after every long flight. The trouble taken to care for the sparking plugs was amply repaid, though it necessitated the constant attention of two mechanics.

On June 4th, twelve machines, with two emergency machines, led by Capts. Thom and Taylor, set out for Thionville or Hagondange. The two emergency machines returned after seeing twelve machines across the Lines, but unfortunately two others were compelled to return shortly afterwards, Lieut. Beecroft with a broken oil pipe, and Lieut. Marshall with a cracked cylinder head. There was a very strong N.E. wind and almost continuous clouds, with a small gap over Metz. Bombs were accordingly dropped on Metz Sablon, the results being unobserved.

The next day the Squadron moved to Azelot, about eight miles south of Nancy, on to an excellent aerodrome, but into temporary accommodation, with the officers' camp, men's camp, and hangars considerably scattered. A raid was attempted, but the wind was found too strong to carry it out.

Engine trouble again defeated the Squadron on the 6th, only eleven machines of "A" and "B" Flights actually getting into the air, of which six finally returned without crossing the Lines. The remaining five machines, under Capt. Thom, reached Thionville Station, which was bombed through a gap in thick clouds. Observations of results were impossible.

The next day's work was even more depressing, as only four machines reached Thionville, under Capt. Purser, out of the twelve which started from "B" and "C" Flights. Several machines, including Capt. Taylor's, which burst the radiator, returned with various engine troubles, and the remainder failed to get together owing to misunderstanding as to formation places. The accuracy of the bombing was excellent, a direct hit being obtained on a road bridge opposite the Station and several others on or alongside the railway.

On June 8th, two formations of six machines each, led by Capts. Thom and Taylor, started for Thionville, of which nine eventually bombed Hagondange through a gap in thick clouds which covered the country further north. Results were unobserved. Of

JUNE 8TH

the five machines which returned with their bombs, Capt. Taylor's broke the magneto drive ; Lieut. Richards' engine would not give satisfactory results at a height ; and Lieuts. Freeland's and Black's developed some sort of ignition trouble. Lieut. Garrity was forced to return owing to faintness in the air, probably largely due to the unsuitable position of the exhaust outlets in line with the pilot's face

The formations were very good indeed. Brig.-General Newall told the Squadron-Commander that he had never seen better formations than those of this raid, when they passed over Brigade Headquarters about ten minutes before crossing the Lines.

The first target in Germany proper was attacked on June 9th. Thirteen machines, including one emergency machine, left to bomb Dillingen in the Saar Valley, 41 miles over the Lines ; of these all the twelve detailed reached the objective, which consisted of a large steel works with two sets of blast furnaces. Excellent results were obtained, two hits being reported on the south portion of the factory, three on the railway close by, three on the Station, and two in the town. The positions of several of these bursts were shown by photographs. The raid formations were led by Capt. Thom and Lieut. Beecroft, who took over "B" Flight in the absence of Capt. Purser. The Squadron received congratulations from Major-General Sir H. M. Trenchard, K.C.B., D.S.O., Commanding the Independent Force R.A.F., and also from the Brig.-General. During the last few raids no opposition from hostile machines had been encountered.

Lieut. Garrity, who had been suffering from breathing difficulty in the air, was sent to Hospital and struck off strength. Capt. Purser, who was also suffering from breathing difficulty, caused by a wound in the lungs, was forbidden by the Medical Officer to continue high flying.

On the next day the weather rendered operations impossible. There was an enormous amount of work to be done on engines and aeroplanes. One machine had to be rebuilt as a result of anti-aircraft fire. Besides the usual routine of changing broken valve springs and cleaning sparking plugs, the following work had to be undertaken by Flights :

HISTORY OF 99 SQUADRON

"*A*" *Flight* dismantled one engine to grind in a burnt valve, and took down the cooling system of another which was overheating badly.

"*B*" *Flight* fitted one new engine and took off the cylinders of another to replace a burnt valve.

"*C*" *Flight* fitted one new engine, and also replaced a burnt valve and thoroughly inspected one engine which had never given satisfactory results since delivered to the Squadron. At this time there was a considerable amount of sickness in the Squadron, and about twenty other ranks were off duty for this reason.

On June 11th the weather was again bad, but some useful formation practice was accomplished.

On the next day the weather was very bad up till 4 p.m., when a raid, led by Capts. Taylor and Beecroft, left to bomb Metz Sablon through gaps in the clouds. Twelve machines reached the objective, most of the bombs falling on or near the Barracks, S.W. of the Triangle.

Lieuts. Vick and Underwood performed their first duties over the Lines.

On June 15th, Dillingen was attacked for the second time, by "A" and "C" Flights. Of the fourteen machines which started, ten actually dropped bombs and returned safely. The two formations of five were led by Capt. Thom and Lieut. Papenfus, the latter having taken over from Capt. Taylor, who was compelled to return with a broken magneto drive. The two formations separated to bomb. "A" Flight obtained very good effect on or near the Railway Station, reporting three direct hits on the line just south of the Station, two just east of the line on some buildings, and one in an open space just S.E. of the Station. These were confirmed by a photograph (99 D.A. 50), which shows the latter as causing what appear to be very large flames. It was later reported by the local inhabitants that this bomb had burst a large watermain.

"C" Flight's results were not confirmed by photographs. Observers were unanimous in stating that all the bombs burst within the precincts of the Factory, the majority falling on the north bank of the river, where a direct hit was obtained on the furnaces. One

DILLINGEN.

direct hit was claimed on the blast furnaces to the south of the river. This raid showed a considerable improvement in engine running, as the failures on three out of four machines which did not reach the objective were caused by broken parts.

Lieut. Papenfus was later awarded the Distinguished Flying Cross for the general excellence of his work, and in particular for his sound leadership on this raid. Lieut. Melville rejoined from Hospital, having almost recovered from his wound.

An attempt was made to reach Metz on the afternoon of the 16th, but formations were compelled to return owing to thick clouds at 3000 feet.

Continuous rain stopped all flying on Monday the 17th. Work on machines and engines was now well in hand, as considerable experience had been gained, and repairs were consequently done much more quickly.

On the 18th and 19th bad weather again stopped operations, and only a few tests and practice flights could be carried out. An interesting improvement was effected on D.H. 9 No. 6202, which had never given a satisfactory performance. It was noticed that this was one of several machines fitted with small size air intake pipes to the carburettors. The original pipes of 1-7/8 inches internal diameter were changed for those of 2-7/8 inches, and a considerable improvement obtained. On the same day, with full load of bombs, under exactly similar conditions, the climb was 3000 feet in seven minutes with the small pipes, and 3000 feet in 5-1/4 minutes, and 6000 feet in 14 minutes with the larger size. The latter was a good average performance for a D.H. 9 with full service load.

Bad weather continued over the 20th, 21st, 22nd and 23rd. Mechanics obtained a much-needed rest after the last few weeks, during which the average daily working hours had been not less than fourteen.

Capt. Purser was struck off the Squadron's strength on transfer to the Home Establishment, and Lieut. Beecroft promoted Captain to command "B" Flight in his place.

Towards evening the weather cleared a little, and two Flights, under Capts. Thom and Beecroft, dropped bombs on Metz Sablon, but results could not be observed owing to clouds.

HISTORY OF 99 SQUADRON

The weather was very cloudy on the 24th, but two formations, led by Capts. Taylor and Beecroft respectively, set out to bomb Dillingen. "C" Flight found their objective and bombed through a small gap in the clouds, being unable to observe results. The leader lost his way on the return journey, and the formation finally landed after being in the air for over 4-1/2 hours.

Capt. Beecroft with "B" Flight was unable to see Dillingen, so bombs were dropped on Saarbrucken, which was visible through a gap, a few bursts being observed on the railway and town. Ten machines completed the raid out of the twelve detailed.

Offenburg Station and sidings, 45 miles over the Lines, were bombed for the first time by "A" and "C" Flights. Three machines dropped out of formation before crossing the Lines ; Lieuts. Freeland and West with minor engine trouble, and Lieut. Underwood feeling unwell. The remaining machines reached their objective, where they were attacked by seven hostile scouts whilst bombs were being dropped. Lieut. Harper, with Lieut. Benson as observer, had his engine disabled in the course of the fight, and was last seen going down under control in the Rhine Valley. Lieut. Jenkin, who was flying with Lieut. Sanders, was hit in the head by a piece of anti-aircraft shell-case, and was dead when lifted out of the machine on return to the aerodrome. These were very serious losses for the Squadron.

Four direct hits on the sidings were reported, of which one on the track and one in the Goods Yard were shown in a photograph (99 D.A. 60). The bursts were reported as scattered, one having hit the Barracks a considerable distance from the objective. This was probably accounted for by the hostile attack at the time of bombing. The Squadron was now reduced to only fifteen pilots available for duty over the Lines, there being considerable sickness at this time.

The next day twelve machines left at 10 a.m. for Karlsruhe. Capt. Thom and Lieut. Sanders, in the absence of Capt. Beecroft through sickness, led the two formations ; but five of the latter's formation did not cross the Lines, and the sixth filled a gap in "A" Flight's formation. The following pilots were compelled to return for various reasons :—Lieut. Sanders, with a cracked cylinder head ;

BURSTS ON SIDINGS AT OFFENBURG

Lieut. Chapin, owing to his observer, Lieut. Taylor, having fainted in the air ; Lieut. Vick, with a loose small-end bearing ; and Lieuts. Richards, Black, and Whattam with minor engine trouble, which prevented their keeping in place. The following pilots and observers completed the raid successfully :—
> Capt. Thom and Lieut. Claye.
> Lieuts. Freeland and Sothcott.
> Lieuts. Marshall and Bell.
> Lieuts. Papenfus and Benjamin.
> Lieuts. West and Levy.
> Lieuts. Thompson and Thornley.

Bursts were difficult to observe, but several were reported on and about the Station. There were a considerable number of hostile machines in the air, most of which attacked the formation of 104 Squadron. On this raid an attempt was made to combine with 104 Squadron's formations, but this was entirely unsuccessful owing to the different ideas of rendezvous in the two Squadrons, and the difference in cruising speed when in formation. At this time the average true air-speed, flying level at 13,000 feet, for formations of 99 Squadron was about 76 miles per hour with bombs, and 85 miles per hour without bombs.

A second combined raid with 104 Squadron was carried out on Thionville Railway Works, 99 Squadron's formations being led by Capts. Taylor and Beecroft. The combination was rather more satisfactory than on the previous day, but again revealed considerable differences of method in the two Squadrons. The formations of 55 Squadron also took part, flying above the D.H. 9's. Out of thirteen machines which left the ground eleven bombed the objective. The results could not be accurately observed, owing to clouds and the presence of enemy aircraft. Shortly after leaving the objective a most determined attack was made on "B" Flight by about 12 E.A., Albatross scouts, Fokker triplanes, and Phaltz scouts, the enemy diving in to about twenty yards' range at times. Lieut. Singleton, flying with Lieut. Black, shot down one of the enemy, which broke in the air ; and Lieut. Walker, with Lieut. Sanders, brought down another in flames. The destruction of both these machines was confirmed by observers of 55 Squadron, who were on the raid. Lieut. Walker was shortly afterwards awarded the Distinguished Flying Cross for the excellent manner in which he conducted himself during this engagement, as well as for the ability which he displayed in his work as observer on all occasions. The Squadron lost Lieuts. Chapin and Wiggins, whose machine went down in flames. Lieut. Sanders was shot through the leg, below the knee, but brought his machine back safely to the aerodrome.

On the 28th, the weather was hopelessly cloudy till the evening, when a raid on Erescaty Aerodrome was attempted, but had to be abandoned owing to clouds and mist.

The Squadron was now very much below strength in flying personnel available for raids, as, besides the recent casualties, Lieuts. Vick and Underwood were unfit for further service flying ; Lieut. Whattam was ill ; Lieut. Broadbent away on special leave ; and Sergt Wilson had not yet finished his training in formation flying, though showing great promise. The following pilots reported for duty :—2nd Lieuts. F. Smith, L. V. Dennis, F. T. Cockburn, C. D. Clark, and W. C. Francis.

The next day the weather was unfit for service flying. A considerable amount of work was done by new pilots, as the machines were now in good order. The latest arrivals were taken up as passengers with the senior pilots of the Squadron on a demonstration of formation flying; as it had been found in the past that new pilots could not be easily impressed with the idea of really close flying. A great many practice flights were accomplished, a most valuable day's work. Lieut. Francis was medically inspected, passed unfit for high flying, and transferred to the Home Establishment. The problem now before the Squadron was to bring on the new pilots quickly, as the casualties received in action and due to sickness had far outrun the effective reinforcements. This presented considerable difficulty, as none of those who joined at this time had done useful formation flying in England. On this day Lieuts. Vick and Levy were lost to the Squadron owing to sickness.

On the 30th, Capts. Thom and Taylor started for Hagenau Aerodrome, leading two formations of five machines, all available

Off the Target, Hagenau Aerodrome.

pilots being employed. Of these, only six finally bombed the target, obtaining a number of hits on the aerodrome clear of the hangars.

Lieut. Richards returned owing to sickness in the air, the beginning of a severe attack of influenza; Lieut. West with magneto trouble; and Lieuts. Black and Whattam with minor engine troubles, which prevented their keeping up to the formation. This was another example of the lack of reserve power of the B.H.P. D.H. 9 at bombing height with full load.

The following reported for duty :—As pilots—2nd Lieuts. G. Martin, T. M. Ritchie, and C. W. Hewson; as observers— Sergts. J. Jones, F. L. Lee, and H. S. Bynon.

On the 1st of July, all available pilots, with the exception of one Flight Commander for training duty, were sent up, ten machines, under Capts. Thom and Beecroft, leaving to bomb the railway sidings and junction at Konz, south of Treves, about sixty miles over the Lines. Unfortunately four machines again dropped out; Capt. Taylor was compelled to bring back his observer, Lieut. Sothcott, who fainted in the air; Lieut. Whattam felt sick in the air, and was admitted to hospital and struck off strength; a plug from the bottom of one carburettor fell off Lieut. Black's machine before he crossed the Lines; and Sergt. Wilson, who was on his first duty, was signalled away so as to leave a standard six formation.

The following pilots reached Konz and returned safely under the leadership of Capt. Thom :—Capt. Beecroft, Lieuts. Marshall, Thompson, Papenfus and West.

Excellent results were obtained in spite of almost continuous fighting. On the way out a formation of four E.A. attacked seriously three times, five attacked over the objective, and five on the return journey. Lieut. Connell was wounded in the wrist, and did not return to the Squadron from Hospital. On this raid the formation flying was excellent throughout, and its success was undoubtedly due to the admirable leadership of Capt. Thom and the steadiness of all pilots in action, as well as to the sound fire tactics of the observers. The report of bombing results was unfortunately unconfirmed, as the machine which carried a camera did not cross the Lines.

On July 2nd, Capt. Thom again led a formation of six machines to Konz. In all, nine machines left the ground, these being flown by the only available pilots in the Squadron. Of these Capt. Taylor returned, as his observer, Lieut. Munson, fainted in the air; Lieut. West, with a loose petrol tap; and Lieut. Broadbent, with ignition trouble. The formation was heavily attacked over Konz, and Capt. Thom, not wishing to risk inaccurate bombing whilst engaged with the enemy, proceeded to Treves, where the Station was bombed after the attack had been beaten off. The majority of the bombs fell in the town near the Station, results not being confirmed by photographs. In the course of fighting over Konz and on the return journey, good formation flying again stopped the enemy, and no casualties were suffered. One hostile scout was driven down under control into a large wood by Lieut. Claye, flying with Capt. Thom. In order to draw the enemy into the air two hours before the bombing formation crossed the Lines, a practice raid of one formation from 99 and one from 104 Squadron had been sent up two hours in advance to climb to bombing height and fly to the Lines west of Pont a Mousson on the Moselle. This manœuvre was apparently successful, as the bombers encountered no opposition till over the objective, whereas on the previous day attacks had commenced almost as soon as the Lines had been crossed.

In recognition of his excellent leadership on this raid, as well as his previous good work, Captain Thom was awarded the Distinguished Flying Cross.

On this day Lieut. W. J. Garrity returned to the Squadron from Hospital.

On the next day the weather was unfit for operations. There was a considerable amount of rigging work to be done, as the machines had been severely damaged during the fighting of the preceding day. At this time the engines were in good order, and the fitters had their work well in hand. Four practice formations of three machines each were carried out. Lieuts. Thompson and Freeland were sent to Hospital with influenza, which was raging at this time.

The German night-bombers appeared to have been reinforced, as there were a considerable number flying over or near Azelot each

JULY 3RD

fine night from this time onwards. This was very annoying, as precautionary measures were necessary, which frequently entailed the Squadron's standing-by in the trenches near the camp, and thus losing sleep.

Number of flights for test or practice—17.

On July 4th the weather was very bad, and only one practice formation was carried out.

On the next day only seven pilots were available for a raid. These left to bomb Kaiserslautern, accompanied by a formation from 104 Squadron. Unfortunately the latter broke up owing to the leader's engine having seized. Of 99 Squadron's formation Lieut. West returned with ignition trouble before crossing the Lines. Capt. Thom led the remainder to Saarbrucken, as the weather proved too cloudy to reach Kaiserslautern. Over the objective a most determined attack was made simultaneously from front and rear by eight hostile machines, which came to very short range. These were successfully driven off, and all our machines returned to the aerodrome. The Squadron suffered a great loss in the death of Lieut. Claye, Capt. Thom's observer, who was killed in the fight. Capt. Thom was fortunate to escape, as he was bruised severely in the arm by a bullet, and his machine was so badly damaged that it was necessary to rebuild it. Both pilots and observers were able to use their guns at short range, and Lieut. Taylor, with Capt. Beecroft, shot down one E.A., of which the wings folded together. Lieut. Bell, with Lieut. Marshall, brought down another out of control. The pilots and observers engaged on this raid were as follows :—

  Capt. Thom and Lieut. Claye.
  Capt. Beecroft and Lieut. Taylor.
  Lieuts. Stevenson and Walker.
  Lieuts. Marshall and Bell.
  Lieut. Broadbent and Sergt. Jones.
  Sergts. Wilson and Lee.

On July 6th the weather was unfit for operations till late in the evening. A successful raid with six machines was carried out on Metz Sablon, results being unobserved owing to clouds. The formation was attacked by eight hostile machines over the objective, and Sergt Wilson's machine was hit in the radiator. He landed, not far from Azelot, in a very rough grass field, and broke his undercarriage. Four practice formations were carried out.

On the next day a six formation, with one emergency machine, led by Capt. Thom, left to bomb Kaiserslautern, with a formation of 104 Squadron. Immediately after taking off, Capt. Taylor's engine stopped, and he landed in a corn field, running into a ditch and breaking his machine. The remainder reached the objective and returned successfully. The bombing was very effective, a direct hit being obtained on the railway, several alongside the Station, and others on buildings in the vicinity. Eight or ten hostile scouts attacked on the return journey, concentrating principally on 104's formation. One was shot down out of control by the latter. There were no decisive results of the fighting with 99's formation.

Lieut. Stevenson was later awarded the Distinguished Flying Cross in recognition of the general excellence of his work, and, in particular, of his admirable skill and steadiness in formation during this raid.

At the time the Squadron was getting excellent results from the B.H.P. engines, although there were many cases of broken cylinder heads. The riggers were kept very busy, as a great many planes had to be changed after being damaged in combat. Lieuts. Underwood, Rimmer, and Whattam were struck off the Squadron's strength on admission to Hospital.

Lieut. P. Dietz, of the U.S.A. Aviation Section, reported for duty as pilot on July 5th.

On July 8th, Capt. Taylor led a successful raid of six machines to Buhl Aerodrome, approximately 18 miles over the Lines, the weather having become fit for flying at about 3.45 p.m. A direct hit was reported on the largest permanent hangar in the N.E. corner of the aerodrome, and also on a smaller building at its southern end. A hit on or beside the hangar is confirmed by a photograph (99 D.A. 69), which shows a large mass of white smoke over the southern portion. Another burst is shown on the aerodrome about 100 yards in front of the hangars, and three wide of the target.

BUHL AERODROME, A BURST ON OR BESIDE THE LARGEST SHED.

Destruction of Thionville Goods Station. (1) A Direct Hit on an Ammunition Train.

JULY 8TH

On this day three practice formations were carried out, formation practice being, in view of the shortage of experienced pilots, almost as important as service flying.

Azelot Aerodrome was bombed for the first time. Two M.T. drivers were hit, of whom 2/A.M. T. J. Jeffrey had to be sent to Hospital with a serious wound in the shoulder.

On the next day the weather was unfit for bombing, and only two practice formations were carried out.

On July 10th the weather was unfavourable, with a very strong wind and continuous clouds at about 4000 feet. Some very useful formation practice was accomplished.

Lieut. Freeland was admitted to Hospital sick, and was struck off the strength of the Squadron.

On the next day the weather was totally unfit for flying. Second Lieuts. M. A. Dunn, F. W. Woolley, H. W. Batty and Sergts. F. Coulson and V. Foulsham reported for duty as observers.

On July 12th, 13th and 14th no operations were detailed, owing to shortage of supplies, due to strikes in England. A considerable amount of valuable practice flying was done on these days with pilots under training :—Lieuts. Cockburn and Clark of "A" Flight ; Lieuts. Dennis, Martin, Ritchie and Hewson of "B" Flight ; Lieuts. Dietz and Smith, and Sergt. Adcock, of "C" Flight.

On Monday, the 15th, a raid on Buhl Aerodrome was detailed. Thirteen machines left the ground, of which only six eventually bombed the objective. Of the seven machines which returned before crossing the Lines, Lieut. Sothcott was ill in the air on one, and the engine on another had a badly cracked cylinder head. The remainder were affected by the usual broken valve springs and minor defects.

Some very useful formation practice was accomplished.

Lieut. J. K. Speed, of the U.S.A. Aviation Section, reported for duty as observer.

Capts. Thom and Beecroft led two formations, of six machines each, to Thionville, and bombed the Station in a strong west wind, followed shortly afterwards by two formations of 55 Squadron. This raid was, as regards material damage, the most effective carried out by the Squadron. Four or five bombs are shown bursting on trains on the main railway line in photographs taken at the time (99 D.A. 77 and 80). Observers of both 55 and 99 Squadrons reported enormous explosions in the Goods Station, the smoke and flames of which could be seen from a distance of about twenty miles. A photograph (99 D.A. 83) taken on the next day shows a great change in the aspect of the Station and sidings. The amount of rolling stock has been reduced by about half, and the lines, at the point where the bombs fell, are clear save for scattered objects, which cannot be recognised. Two very large sheds or warehouses on the north side of the line opposite the Fort have completely disappeared, leaving white marks, which seem to be large holes in the ground. Further to the north, between the railway and the river, another large building has also disappeared. After the Armistice an inspection of the damage and of photographs taken locally at this time confirms the fact of a vast quantity of munitions having blown up and completely destroyed the Goods Station.*

Repatriated prisoners of war made the following report on the condition of the railway after this raid: "The train, on which we were, left the Station at Thionville just after the raid on the 16th of July. Owing to all traffic being stopped for about forty hours, the trains were diverted and sent via Longuyon, Audun-le-Roman, and Metz. We saw ten engines damaged by bombs lying to the side of the line and many wrecked carriages. We noticed that the passenger station on the left of the line had not sustained any damage, but that the buildings of the Goods Station had been completely wrecked. Between the Goods Station and the line followed by our train there were three or four sidings damaged by the explosion."

The Squadron lost the services of 2nd Lieut. Sothcott, who was admitted to Hospital with appendicitis on this day.

On the 17th, Thionville was again raided in a strong west wind, probably 35 miles per hour, at 12,000 feet. The weather was very hot and a great deal of overheating of the engines resulted, only six machines reaching the objective. The formation was led by Capt. Thom. The bombing was accurate, considering the strength

* See photographs facing pages 28, 29 and 30.

Destruction of Thionville Goods Station. (2) The Smoke Spreading.

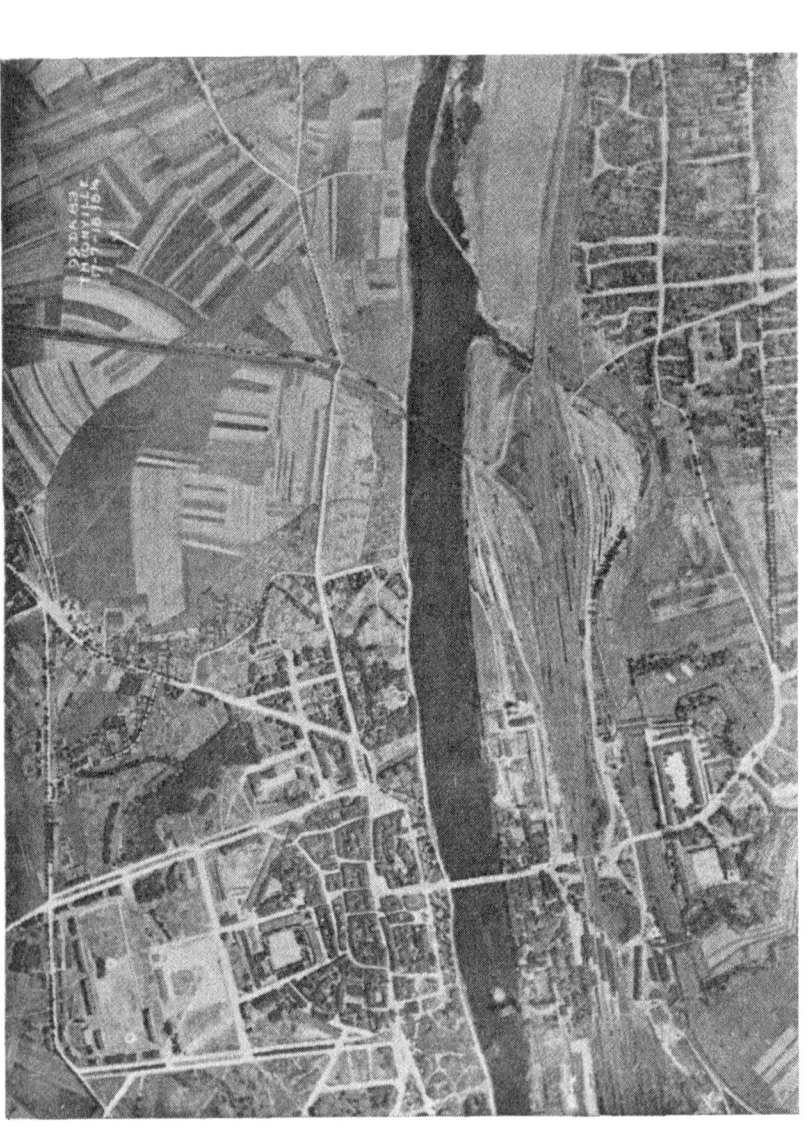

Thionville, 17/7/18, showing Rolling Stock removed from Sidings and space where Warehouses stood in Goods Station

of the wind and the volume and accuracy of the anti-aircraft fire always encountered over this target. Several bursts are shown along the south bank of the river near the Station in a photograph (99 D.A. 83); and the observers reported all the bombs as being grouped in that area. Lieut. F. K. Crosbie-Choppin, with 2nd Lieuts. W. Hodder and E. L. McCowen, reported for duty as pilots.

On July 18th the weather was totally unfit for flying. A useful day's work was carried out, as most of the aeroplanes and engines needed considerable attention after the great amount of service and practice flying, which had been recently accomplished.

On the next day the weather was again unfit for operations, and only a limited amount of practice flying was possible. After having been much under strength in effective pilots for a considerable period, "C" Flight carried out a successful formation practice with six machines.

On July 20th, the wind was too strong from the west for the long raid to Stuttgart, for which the Squadron was standing-by at this time. A considerable amount of valuable practice flying was, however, carried out.

The wind was less strong on July 21st, and an attempt was made by "A" and "C" Flight formations to reach Stuttgart.

Of the fourteen machines which left the ground, ten actually bombed Offenburg, the wind having proved too strong to reach Stuttgart. Lieut. Dietz swung badly when taking off, and his machine hit a hangar. Capt. Thom dropped out of his formation, owing to a defect in the petrol system, and Lieuts. Stevenson and Cockburn returned with ignition trouble before crossing the Lines. Lieut. Doidge took over leadership of "A" Flight formation, and obtained excellent results on the sidings at Offenburg, two bombs being reported as bursting on or very near a large engine shed, and several others on the line. The bursts from "C" Flight's bombs were unobserved. Twenty enemy aircraft attacked over the objective, showing considerable determination, but were driven off, the new pilots on this raid showing great steadiness and flying in excellent formation. Lieuts. Thompson and Thornley were unfortunately taken prisoners, their machine being seen to go down under control, with a punctured radiator, when recrossing the Rhine. No decisive results on the enemy could be claimed with certainty owing to the confusion and closeness of the fighting.

In the course of the fighting, 2nd Lieut. T. K. Ludgate was wounded in the hand. He was struck off the Squadron's strength on admission to Hospital.

On the 22nd, the wind was again blowing strongly from the west, dropping somewhat in the afternoon. "A" and "B" Flights left at 2.20 p.m. on another attempt to reach Stuttgart, but finding the wind still very strong, again bombed Offenburg. Twelve machines reached the objective, and excellent results were obtained, the majority of the bombs hitting the sidings and Station, and only one bursting clear of the objective and buildings in the vicinity. Two excellent photographs (99 D.A. 93 and 94) confirmed the reported accuracy of the bombing, and show one or more bursts on or beside the main buildings of the Passenger Station; three or four bursts spread across the lines just south of the Passenger Station; one on the end of a road-bridge over the railway; two more on or beside the line, and several in the town near the Station.

Just after dropping their bombs the formations were attacked by 16 hostile scouts. Of these, one was shot down by Lieut. Woolley and Sergt. Lee flying respectively with Lieut. Dennis and Sergt. Wilson. In the course of the fight the machines of Lieuts. Smith and Broadbent were disabled with bullets through the radiators. They were followed down towards the Lines by the enemy, and both came down just clear of the Lines near Raon l'Etape in the Vosges. Lieut. Broadbent was probably saved by the dash with which Capt. Thom dived on to the pursuing enemy. Lieut. Smith landed on a very steep hill among tall fir trees, leaving most of the fabric parts of his machine hanging on the branches and burying its engine in the soft ground. Neither pilot or observer was injured by the fall, though Sergt. Coulson had been wounded in the arm during the fight. Owing to the steepness of the hills, only the engine of this machine could be salved, and that was considerably damaged in transport as well as by the fall. Lieut. Broadbent and Sergt. Jones landed in a very narrow valley among the foot-hills, with little

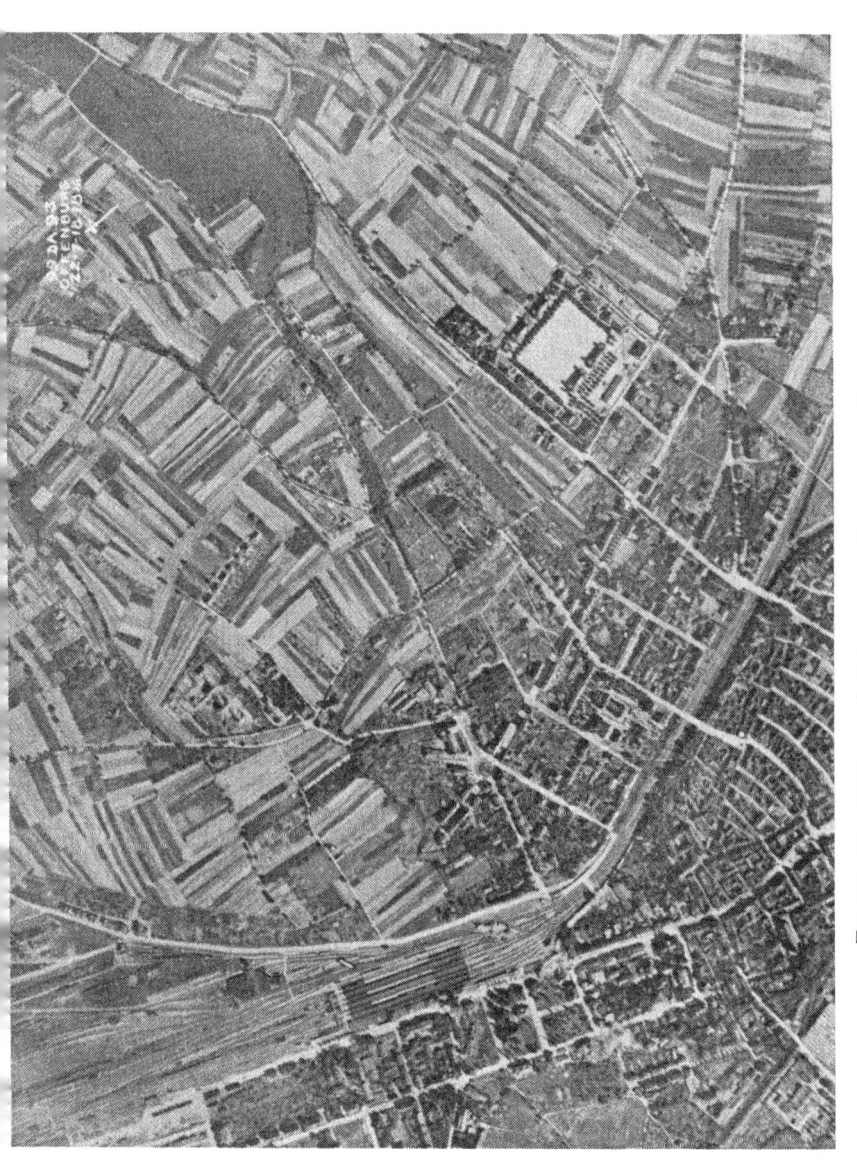

Bombs bursting on Station and Sidings at Offenburg.

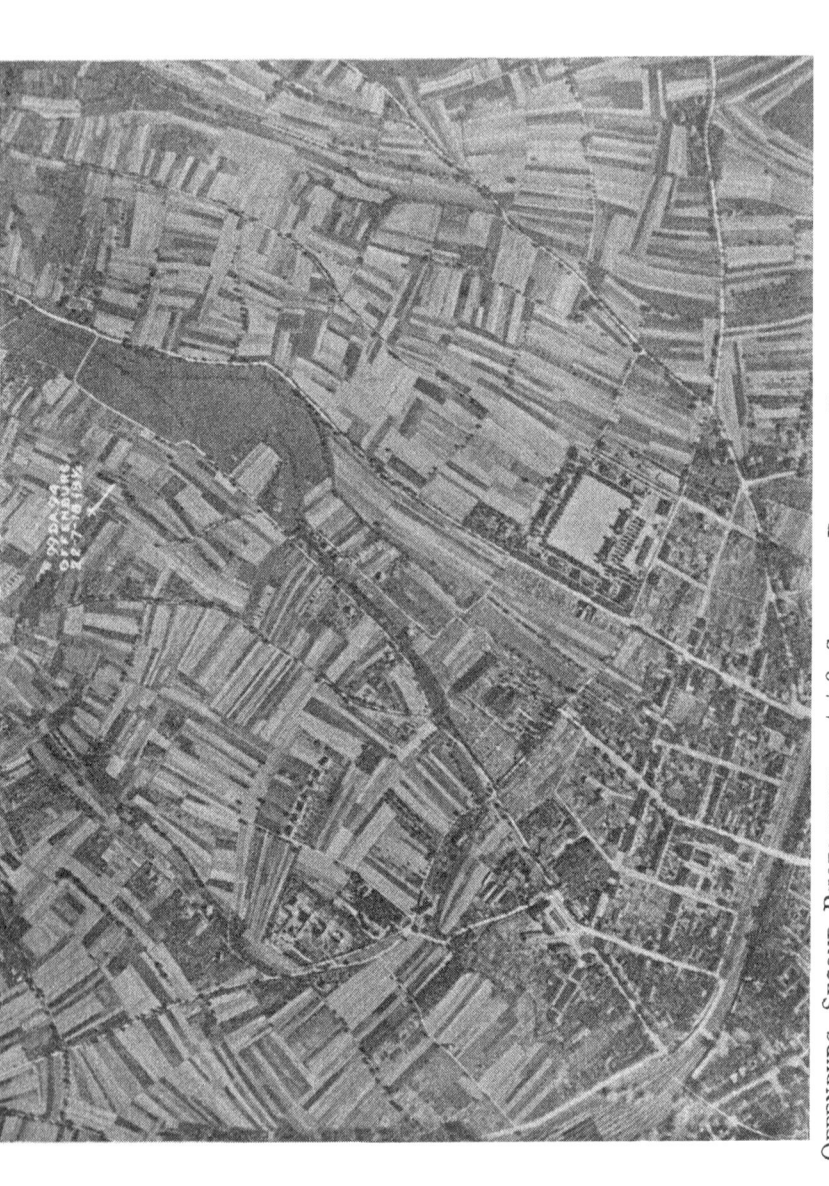

Offenburg, Second Photograph, 22/7/18, Showing Burst on Bridge crossing the Railway.

Face page 27]

damage to their machine. It is recorded that they did not know whether they were on the German or French side of the Lines, and ran to cover in case the Germans appeared. For a few minutes they waited in trepidation, but were finally reassured by hearing an irritated voice remark, " Where have those gard-damned aviators gone." The greatest possible assistance was given by the local American units in salving these machines and returning the pilots and observers to the Squadron. On this day Sergt. Adcock (pilot) was transferred to the Home Establishment, and Sergt. Bynon admitted to Hospital sick. The following observers reported for duty :—Lieuts. H. G. Ramsay, S. G. Burton, H. E. Alsford, K. H. Ashton, L. W. G. Stagg, A. T. Bower, and G. E. Stephenson.

On the next day the weather was quite unfit for flying, with strong wind and rain.

Bad weather continued over the 24th, when, however, some practice flying was accomplished.

On July 25th, the weather was again unfit for service flying. Some useful practice work was done.

By this date new pilots had been trained to replace the losses incurred during June and the beginning of July, and the Squadron formation flying was excellent. There was still considerable difficulty in obtaining sufficient D.H. 9's as replacements, to keep up to effective strength. The standing arrangement of personnel in flight formations was, at this time, as follows :—

"A" Flight

(*Leader*) CAPT. THOM (Pilot)
LIEUT. MELVILLE (Observer)

(*Left Front*)
LIEUT. STEVENSON
LIEUT. SPEED

(*Right Front*)
LIEUT. MARSHALL
LIEUT. BELL

(*Deputy Leader*) LIEUT. DOIDGE
LIEUT. WALKER

(*Left Rear*)
LIEUT. BROADBENT
SERGT. JONES

(*Right Rear*)
LIEUT. WEST
LIEUT. DUNN

(*Spare Machine*) LIEUT. CLARK
LIEUT. BOWER

"B" Flight
(*Leader*) CAPT. BEECROFT (Pilot)
LIEUT. TAYLOR (Observer)

(*Left Front*)
SERGT. WILSON
SERGT. LEE

(*Deputy Leader*) LIEUT. GARRITY
LIEUT. BEALE

(*Left Rear*)
LIEUT. BLACK
LIEUT. SINGLETON

(*Spare Machine*) LIEUT. RITCHIE
LIEUT. STAGG

(*Right Front*)
LIEUT. HEWSON
LIEUT. ALSFORD

(*Right Rear*)
LIEUT. DENNIS
LIEUT. WOOLLEY

"C" Flight
(*Leader*) CAPT. TAYLOR (Pilot)
LIEUT. NOTLEY (Observer)

(*Left Front*)
LIEUT. RICHARDS
LIEUT. MUNSON

(*Deputy Leader*) LIEUT. PAPENFUS
LIEUT. BENJAMIN

(*Left Rear*)
LIEUT. SMITH
LIEUT. ASHTON

(*Right Front*)
LIEUT. MARTIN
LIEUT. BURTON

(*Right Rear*)
LIEUT. DIETZ
LIEUT. BATTY

On July 26th, the weather was again very showery, with low clouds and a strong west wind all day. A little practice flying was accomplished.

The unfavourable weather continued on the 27th and 28th.

On the 29th, the weather improved slightly after 3 p.m., and several practice formations went up.

Early on the 30th, two formations with two emergency machines left for Stuttgart, led by Capts. Taylor and Beecroft. Of these, six left their formations before crossing the Lines, owing to engine trouble and inability to keep up to the leaders at bombing height; Lieut. Black with ignition trouble; Lieut. Clark unable to keep in place in the formation; Lieut. Smith with a defective magneto; Lieuts. Richards, West and Dennis with ignition defects, overheating, and carburettor troubles respectively. Very thick mist rose over the country E. and S.E. of Nancy, which almost completely obscured the ground east of the Vosges. Lieut. Clark was unable to recognise the country after leaving his formation, and finally landed near Dijon.

German Photograph of Destruction of Thionville Goods Station.
(1) Sidings with Remains of Ammunition Train.

German Photograph of Destruction of Thionville Goods Station.
(2) General View of Main Lines and Rolling Stock.

JULY 30TH

Eight pilots dropped bombs on the railway at Lahr, 15 miles S.S.E. of Strasburg, results being unlocated owing to mist. The formations were attacked by twenty hostile machines when recrossing the Rhine. Lieuts. Dietz and Batty were shot down and killed, their machine being seen to break up in the air. Lieut. Martin's machine was disabled by a bullet through the radiator, and his observer, Lieut. Burton, was killed before recrossing the Lines. The pilot was wounded in the foot, but managed to land without a serious crash, in a marsh which appeared through a gap in the mist. His machine was very badly damaged by bullets.

Lieut. Notley, with Capt. Taylor, shot down one E.A. in flames; Lieut. Taylor, with Capt. Beecroft, shot another to pieces; and Sergt. Lee, with Sergt. Wilson, brought down a third, from which the pilot was seen to fall. In addition to the above-named, Lieuts. Hewson and Alsford, Garrity and Melville, and Ritchie and Stagg returned successfully.

Lieut. B. S. W. Taylor was later awarded the Distinguished Flying Cross for the high quality of his work on 19 successful raids, and, in particular, for his coolness and the excellence of his judgment during the intense fighting this day. The excellent fighting qualities of Sergt Lee, which had resulted in his shooting down three hostile machines, were also recognised by an immediate award of the Distinguished Flying Medal.

On Wednesday, the 31st, twelve machines, led by Capt. Taylor and Lieut. Doidge, left for Maintz at 5.30 a.m. Three of these returned before crossing the Lines, Lieut. Broadbent with a cracked cylinder head, and Lieuts. West and Richards with minor engine trouble. The remaining nine machines were attacked by forty hostile scouts in several strong formations in the neighbourhood of Saarburg. The co-operation and power of manœuvre of the enemy were much above the average. Their tactics were to engage in a general combat, six or more machines at a time manœuvring freely above the formation, whilst two or three machines concentrated on a single D.H. 9 from below at very close range. Owing to the fact that the Albatross and Fokker scouts were approximately twenty miles per hour faster than the D.H. 9's, these tactics were practicable, and proved very successful.

Seeing that it would be impossible to reach Maintz in the face of such odds, Capt. Taylor decided to bomb Sarrbrucken. Four D.H. 9's had been shot down before this objective was reached, but the remaining five pilots dropped their bombs on the station and sidings. On the return journey, three more of the formation were put out of action, and it was probably due to the appearance of two formations of 104 Squadron, which had just crossed the Lines, that the remaining machines piloted by Capt. Taylor and Lieut. Hewson, with Lieuts. Notley and Alsford, as observers, were able to regain their aerodrome.

It was afterwards ascertained that the following casualties occurred on this raid :—Lieuts. Doidge and Melville, killed ; Lieuts. Black and Singleton, prisoners ; Lieuts. Smith and Ashton, prisoners; Lieuts. Papenfus and Benjamin, prisoners ; Lieuts. Dennis and Woolley, killed ; Lieut. Ritchie a prisoner, and his observer, Lieut. Stagg, killed ; Lieuts. Garrity and Stephenson, prisoners.

Owing to the intensity of the fighting and the number of machines falling out of the combat it was impossible to ascertain the enemy's casualties.

The formation flying was good throughout the engagement, and the greatest credit was due to the pilots and observers for their steadiness under such hopeless conditions. This fight again revealed the disadvantageous position of the D.H. 9 radiator under the fuselage. This increased the size of the vulnerable target by at least one-third for an enemy attacking from behind and below.

These severe losses made it impossible for the Squadron to muster enough pilots and observers for a raid till reinforcements had been trained up to the necessary standard in formation flying. The feeling of despondence which was naturally felt on this day was considerably relieved by the great sympathy and kindness shown towards the remnant of the Squadron by the senior officers of the Independent Force. In spite of the great press of work during that period, General Trenchard found time to spend several hours with

German Photograph of Destruction of Thionville Goods Station.
(3) Site of Two Very Large Warehouses.

the Squadron; and General Newall and Lieut.-Colonel Baldwin arrived in the afternoon and stayed to dinner.

On August 1st, the Squadron settled down to a very busy period of reconstruction and training, practice formations being arranged each evening and machines allotted to pilots in the same way as for operations. The majority of the pilots who had recently joined the Squadron had done practically no formation flying in England.

Lieuts. W. T. Jones and J. L. Hunter reported for duty as pilots; and Lieut. E. G. Black, of the U.S. Aviation Section, and 2nd Lieut. W. Shaw as observers.

On this day five practice formations of three machines each, led by experienced pilots, were carried out.

On the next day the weather was quite unfit for flying. At this time Lieut. Stevenson assumed command of "A" Flight, in the absence of Capt. Thom on leave. This Flight had been commanded by Lieut. Doidge for a few days before his death on July 31st.

On August 3rd, a most useful day's practice flying was done, all new pilots taking part in at least two practice formations. The Squadron had now been reinforced up to 15 machines, but was still much below establishment in pilots.

Second Lieut. Cockburn left the Squadron on returning to England.

On the next day the weather was very bad for flying, and only two machines left the ground.

The weather improved slightly on August 5th, and a number of practice formations were carried out, in which considerable improvement was shown; but on the 6th, conditions were again very unfavourable.

On the 7th, the sky was covered by low clouds almost all day. The more experienced pilots commenced practice in flying through clouds, in which great difficulty was experienced owing to the shortage of this type of training received by them whilst in England. The new pilots were again busily employed on formation practice.

The same kind of work was again undertaken with energy on he 8th, under similar weather conditions.

Numerous reinforcements arrived on August 9th, most of whom were very ill-trained for the work of a day-bombing Squadron, having been hurried through their training in England without adequate instruction in formation flying or map-reading.

The following reported for duty on this day :—As pilots—2nd Lieuts. R. C. Hardy, G. R. A. Dick, S. Mackeever, M. J. Poulton, D. F. Brooks, W. A. Warwick, and H. E. King. As observers—2nd Lieuts. H. Crossley, R. Buckby, J. C. Barns, E. Smith, J. L. M. Oliphant, T. H. Swann, C. G. Russell, H. A. Boniface, S. Lane, and K. L. Turnbull.

On this and the two succeeding days much valuable practice flying was done, although the weather was still unfit for operations.

The following pilots arrived :—2nd Lieuts. G. W. Irving, E. E. Crosby, and W. J. Baldwin.

On the 12th, there was again great activity in practice, which was, however, rendered somewhat difficult by the number of machines which had been strained by rough landings. The same type of work was carried out on the 13th and 14th, the riggers being kept very busy repairing numerous undercarriages and wheels damaged by the new pilots.

Lieut. Marshall was admitted to Hospital suffering from a severe attack of influenza.

On the 13th, thirteen machines went out on a patrol of the Lines, which had to be abandoned owing to clouds.

On the 15th, the Squadron was detailed for a short raid on Boulay Aerodrome, 32 miles beyond the Lines, with 104 Squadron.

The order that Squadron-Commanders were not to cross the Lines had been cancelled shortly before this, and two operations per month allowed. Major Pattinson took part in his first operation with the Squadron, leading "C" Flight on this raid. Fourteen machines left the ground at about 2.30 p.m. Owing to very hot weather and the inexperience of the new pilots in climbing their machines, only four actually bombed the objective, obtaining a number of hits on the edge of the aerodrome, but clear of the hangars. Owing to the delay in waiting for stragglers, the formation could not keep with those of 104 Squadron, which preceded it.

On the return journey there were a considerable number of hostile scouts in the air, which attacked from long range in pairs and singly till close to the Lines. No decisive results were obtained, but Lieut. Broadbent's machine was very badly damaged by machine-gun fire, and the other machines also hit several times in the fuselages. The four pilots who completed the raid flew in excellent formation, these being Major Pattinson with Lieut. Walker, Lieut. Broadbent with Sergt. Jones, Lieut. Jones with Lieut. Black, and Sergt. Wilson with Sergt. Lee.

General Trenchard telephoned personally to congratulate the Squadron-Commander on having completed the raid successfully after so many machines had failed to cross the Lines.

Second Lieut. Munson was finally ordered to cease flying and was employed as Assistant Recording Officer from this date. A serious accident occurred on this day. When coming down to land, Lieut. MacCowen stalled his machine, which fell from about 200 feet. Both the pilot and his observer, Lieut. Shaw, were severely injured, the former sustaining a broken leg and a broken arm, and the latter grave injuries to one arm and a deep cut in the instep.

For the next three days the Squadron recommenced strenuous training, damage caused to machines by poor landings again hindering work in the air to a considerable extent.

On August 18th, Major Pattinson with Lieut. Walker attempted to reach Dillingen, flying by compass above the clouds, but found the weather unsuitable over the Lines owing to large open spaces in the cloud bank.

On this day, practice flying for inexperienced pilots was curtailed owing to the unfavourable direction of the wind increasing the probability of broken undercarriages.

On August 19th, a very useful day's practice in formation flying was carried out, there being no less than thirty flights for test and practice.

Sergt. Foulsham was transferred to another Squadron, to resume night flying duties.

On August 20th, the weather was unfavourable for service flying in formation, with continuous clouds at a few hundred feet in the morning, which rose to 2000-2500 feet after noon. Major Pattinson with Lieut. Walker left the ground at 1.40 p.m. They climbed through the clouds from 2500 to 5000 feet, above the trenches at Pont-a-Mousson, and reached Dillingen, descending within three miles of the objective after 36 minutes flying by compass over practically unbroken clouds. Two 112 lb. bombs fitted with 15 sec. delay-action fuses were dropped from 2000 feet on the factory, one of which was reported by the observer as having burst on a blast furnace, and caused a very large flash of flame, and the other having hit the railway line which runs round outside the factory.

Anti-aircraft fire was not opened on the machine till after the bombs had exploded, but was then of considerable accuracy for the few seconds before the clouds were re-entered. On the return journey the pilot flew for 45 minutes on an approximate compass course after entering the clouds, and found himself some 10 miles west of Azelot on his descent. The course steered to Dillingen was approximately north-east, and the wind estimated at 25 m.p.h. W.N.W. The enemy were evidently taken by surprise, as no hostile aircraft were seen, and no anti-aircraft fire encountered except over the objective, and not till two or three minutes after the machine had become visible from the ground. The D.H. 9 used for this raid was fitted with a standard 5/17 Creagh-Osborne compass, and no turn indicator was used.

This was the only single machine daylight raid carried out on Germany by a unit of the Independent Force, and also the only daylight raid successfully accomplished by navigation without any sight of landmarks on the route. A telegram of congratulation was received by Major Pattinson from General Trenchard.

Sergt. H. L. Bynon rejoined the Squadron from Hospital.

On the next day some very valuable practice flying was done, the formations showing considerable improvement. The majority of the pilots were at this time very inexperienced. In the absence of Capt. Thom, who was suffering from influenza whilst on leave, and Capt. Beecroft also on leave, "A" and "B" Flights were commanded by Lieuts. Stevenson and Hewson respectively.

AUGUST 21ST

Second Lieuts. L. S. Springett and W. H. Gillett reported for duty as pilots.

Second Lieut. W. J. Baldwin was transferred to the Home Establishment, and Lieut. C. C. Gardner was admitted to Hospital. Lieut. Munson took over the duties of Recording Officer.

On August 22nd, the Squadron was detailed for a raid on Mannheim, as also was 104 Squadron. Only eleven machines were available for this raid. These left the ground in two formations, led by Lieuts. Stevenson and Hewson. The failure of this raid was another example of the weakness of formations of D.H. 9's manned by inexperienced pilots. Lieut. Hewson's formation did not succeed in joining with that of Lieut. Stevenson, and as it was reduced to two machines the leader rightly abandoned the raid. Of the six pilots of "A" Flight, only four crossed the Lines. Seven pilots out of the eleven detailed were thus compelled to return unsuccessfully. Of these Sergt. Wilson alone returned with a serious defect, his petrol supply pipe having become blocked. Of the remaining six, Lieuts. Hewson and Jones abandoned the raid after the remainder of their formation had left them; the other four were unable to keep in place owing to lack of experience and minor faults which could have been overcome by the expert pilot. Lieut. Stevenson, with his formation of four machines, started for Mannheim. When over Hagenau some 25 hostile scouts were sighted flying at about 14,000 feet to the north of the formation. The leader decided that it would be impossible to reach his objective, 60 miles further north, in the face of such heavy odds. Bombs were therefore dropped on Hagenau Aerodrome, results being unobserved. No opposition was encountered on the return journey.

On this day twelve machines of 104 Squadron were very heavily attacked near Mannheim, with the result that seven D.H. 9's were shot down, including the two formation leaders. Lieut. C. J. Kidder, Aviation Section, U.S.A. Army, reported for duty as pilot.

On the next day a great improvement was obtained in engine management on a short raid to Buhl Aerodrome, led by Lieut.

Stevenson and Sergt. Wilson. Eleven machines completed the duty. No direct hits on hangars were reported, though several bombs burst on the aerodrome, and a few not far behind the largest hangar.

On this raid the following pilots and observers completed their first successful duty over the Lines :—Pilots—Lieuts. Brooks, Dick, King, McKeever, and Poulton. Observers—Lieuts. Buckby, Turnbull, Oliphant, Russell, and Lane. Lieut. Marshall was re-posted to the Squadron from Hospital.

On August 24th, the weather was very unsettled, with continuous low clouds. In the afternoon an attempt was made to reach Buhl Aerodrome on a compass course above the clouds by the following pilots and observers :—Capt. Taylor with Lieut. Bell, Lieut. Stevenson and Lieut. Speed, Lieut. Broadbent and Lieut. Walker, Sergt. Wilson and Lieut. Beale. When climbing through the clouds above the Lines a thunderstorm gathered, which compelled the abandonment of the raid.

Whilst returning at about 2000 feet, Capt. Taylor's machine was seen to commence a steep spiral and continue to fall in this manner till it struck the ground. Both Capt. Taylor and Lieut. Bell were dead before help could arrive. The loss of these two officers, who had come overseas with the Squadron, was most deeply felt both in the Squadron's work and amongst those who had served with them. It was thought that Capt. Taylor must have lost consciousness owing to the heat of the day and the bumpiness of the air, combined with the strain of flying through clouds. Although Lieut. Bell was able to control a D.H. 9 from the back seat, there would have been little time to do so before reaching the ground from 2000 feet. These Officers were buried in the Independent Force cemetery just outside the town of Charmes on the Moselle. Lieut. J. W. Richards was transferred to 104 Squadron.

On the 25th, the weather was somewhat more favourable, though clouds still rendered it difficult to distinguish landmarks. A raid on Bettenbourg railway sidings was detailed, formations being led by Lieut. Stevenson and Sergt. Wilson. Owing to the difficulty of locating the target, bombs were dropped on the railway at Arlon,

AUGUST 26TH

25 miles from the Lines. The bursts were unlocated by the observers, but photographs showed several near the railway. Considerable improvement was shown in the running of the engines at bombing height, and twelve pilots dropped bombs and recrossed the Lines. Anti-aircraft fire was reported as heavy and accurate when crossing the trenches in the region of Verdun, where the propeller of Sergt. Wilson's machine was broken, and his engine very badly damaged by a shell. The pilot landed safely near Bar-le-Duc. Four hostile machines were encountered before the bombs were dropped, and seven more on the return journey. These were driven off without decisive results, in spite of the fact that the formation flying was not of the high quality usually displayed. When returning to Azelot, Lieut. Brooks became separated from his formation, and, having lost himself, landed at the American Aerodrome at Colombey-les-Belles, where he unfortunately wrecked his machine.

On the next day the weather was unfavourable for operations, with very low clouds all day. An attempt was made to bomb Buhl Aerodrome, flying by compass above the clouds, but had to be abandoned owing to the great height of some of the clouds and the consequent difficulty of penetrating them and of allowing for the speed of the upper wind. At 2000 feet the wind was 25-30 m.p.h. from the south-west, and therefore very unfavourable for any near objective in the Independent Force area. This raid was attempted by Lieut. Marshall, who had just rejoined the Squadron from leave, and now commanded "C" Flight in place of Capt. Taylor, accompanied by Lieuts. Broadbent and Crosbie-Choppin.

Very useful formation practice was also carried out, seventeen flights being made for this purpose.

Two more pilots arrived for duty :—2nd Lieut. F. A. Wood, Aviation Section, U.S.A. Army, and Lieut. W. E. Ogilvy. 2nd Lieut. K. L. Turnbull was admitted to Hospital sick.

On the morning of the 27th, weather was again unfavourable for service flying. In the late afternoon conditions improved somewhat, though there was a wind of 30-35 m.p.h. from the south. At 4 p.m. eleven machines, all that could be mustered owing to the recent number of forced landings and crashes, left to bomb Buhl

HISTORY OF 99 SQUADRON

Aerodrome in two formations, led by Lieut. Marshall and Sergt. Wilson. The results obtained were very disappointing in view of the recent improvement in the percentage of machines to reach the objective. Lieuts. Crosbie-Choppin, Hodder, and Sergt. Wilson dropped out of their formations with engine trouble, leaving "B" Flight's formation without an experienced pilot as leader. Three more pilots of "B" Flight, Lieuts. King, Kidder and Springett, misunderstood a signal made to them by Lieut. Jones, who had assumed leadership, and also returned before crossing the Lines. The remaining five pilots, Lieuts. Marshall, Dick, Jones, Broadbent and Poulton dropped their bombs on the objective, six bursts being observed on the southern portion of the aerodrome, of which one was within one hundred yards of a hangar. The formation was attacked by six enemy aircraft just before reaching the objective. No decisive results were obtained against the enemy.

Lieut. Broadbent's machine was hit in the radiator in the course of the fight, and he was forced to land near Baggarat, a few miles south of the trenches.

Second Lieut. L. G. Stern reported for duty as pilot.

The wind at 12,000 feet increased to gale force on the 28th, with heavy cloud banks from 5000-10,000 feet. A raid was attempted, thirteen machines leaving at 12.15 p.m., but had to be abandoned owing to the southerly wind of about sixty miles per hour. Twelve of the thirteen machines detailed for this raid attained bombing height in formation, showing considerable improvement on the part of the pilots.

In the afternoon fourteen flights for formation practice were undertaken.

Lieuts. L. G. Dennis and E. A. Bowyer (pilots) arrived.

Lieut. Hewson was struck off the strength on admission to Hospital.

The unfavourable weather continued over the 29th, and no operations were attempted, though useful practice work was continued in the afternoon.

On this day an amusing incident occurred. There had been a thick ground mist over the aerodrome in the morning, which gradually

Buhl Aerodrome with Two Hangars Enveloped in Smoke.

rose to about 500 feet. At noon, when work in the hangars was ceasing for the dinner interval, the local anti-aircraft guns suddenly commenced to fire, and a German Hannoveraner two-seater machine approached the aerodrome flying very low, and losing height, as if about to attack the hangars. As at this time there was considerable discussion as to the possibility of bombing under very low clouds, and, as the hostile machine was obviously too low for anti-aircraft fire to be effective, considerable anxiety was caused. The hostile machine, however, passed over the aerodrome without either dropping bombs or firing, and then flew round at a distance of a few miles. In the meanwhile four French Spad from the neighbouring aerodrome had left the ground, and a Lewis gun had been mounted in the Squadron anti-aircraft gunpit. The German pilot again crossed the aerodrome, and eighty rounds were fired at his machine from about five hundred yards from the Squadron's gun. He then turned south, and finally landed with his engine damaged ten miles south of Azelot after a running fight with the Spads, in the course of which the pilot of one of the latter was killed by a machine-gun bullet through the head. It was ascertained that the German had become lost whilst on a travelling flight to Metz.

On August 30th, the weather was again very cloudy, with a strong south-westerly wind. Fourteen machines, led by Lieuts. Stevenson and Marshall, left the ground at 8.25 a.m. Owing to the thick clouds over the Lines the leaders were compelled to drop their bombs wherever they could see a suitable objective. Six pilots of "A" Flight formation dropped their bombs on Doncourt Aerodrome, near Conflans, where two direct hits were claimed on a hangar in the centre of the aerodrome, and several more beside the hangars, and on what appeared to be a hutted camp. The observers' reports were partially confirmed by photographs, which showed several bursts very near the hangars. "C" Flight's bombs were dropped on the railway junction at Conflans, eighteen miles beyond the Lines. One direct hit and three bursts alongside the railway were reported. Eleven machines completed this raid, Lieut. Hodder returning to the aerodrome with slight engine trouble, which prevented his keeping place in formation, and Sergt. Wilson being forced to land at Amaty Aerodrome S.W. of Toul, owing to a stoppage in the flow of petrol to his engine. Lieut. McKeever's machine was temporarily disabled by a fragment of shell-case in his petrol tank, as the formations were crossing the Lines, which lost him his position in formation. When near Conflans four enemy aircraft attacked at long range from behind. One of these was shot down by Lieut. Lane flying as observer with Lieut. Poulton, and was seen to crash. Lieut. Russell, who was flying with Lieut. Warwick, was unfortunately killed in the course of the combat by a bullet through the head.

Second Lieut. L. B. Duggan joined the Squadron as pilot.

Second Lieut. C. D. Clark was transferred to the Home Establishment.

The weather on August 31st was very cloudy and unsettled, little flying being possible. Shortly after leaving the ground to return to Azelot, Sergt. Wilson's machine stalled, and he and 2nd Lieut. Alsford were killed in the ensuing crash.

In the evening a German night-flying machine dropped a heavy bomb between the Regimental Institute and some Nissen huts in the camp, causing considerable damage. Corpl. J. W. Wymark and A.C. 3rd Class W. Barnard were wounded before they had time to reach the trenches.

The former unfortunately died of his wounds in Hospital.

The weather remained cloudy over the next day, preventing operations. An attempt was made by five pilots to reach Buhl Aerodrome over the clouds, but these were found to be too high, and as the wind was very strong from the west it was thought advisable to abandon the attempt.

Second Lieut. T. M. O'Neill reported for duty as Armament Officer.

On September 2nd, the activities of both day and night-bombing Squadrons were concentrated against two of the most active hostile aerodromes in the forward area, Buhl and Morhange, both within 18 miles of the Lines. The successful part played by 99 Squadron in these raids forms one of the most satisfactory chapters in its history. On Monday, September 2nd, two raids were carried out

BUHL AERODROME, 2/9/18. "A DIRECT HIT."

55 Squadron Photograph Buhl Aerodrome, 2/9/18. Another Hangar Smoking.

by each of the three day-bombing Squadrons of the 41st Wing. Capt. Stevenson led both the raids of 99 Squadron, with Lieut. Marshall as leader of the second formations. Eleven machines successfully completed the first raid, and twelve the second. Just after crossing the Lines on the first occasion, one machine unfortunately dropped out of formation owing to the sudden faintness of the observer, Lieut. Lane. In the morning raid the following results were reported by observers :—One burst from a heavy bomb on the aerodrome between two hostile machines, which were within fifty yards of each other, of which one could not be seen after the smoke had cleared ; two hangars set on fire, and one burst on a small building close behind the largest shed. On the second raid most satisfactory results were again obtained. Observers claimed three direct hits on hangars, one of which was seen to be completely demolished. A good proportion of the bomb-bursts of these two raids were shown on photographs. The results thus confirmed were as follows, the hangars being numbered south from the very large shed for purposes of reference. Photo. 99 D.A. 115 shows No. 9 hangar enveloped in smoke, and obviously on fire ; No. 8 is also apparently on fire. Photo. 99 D.A. 116 confirms the fires in both No. 8 and No. 9, and also shows a huge mass of smoke completely obliterating No. 28 much further to the south. A later photograph shows this hangar as having completely disappeared. Photo. 55 D.A. 2100, which was taken from a machine of No. 55 Squadron passing over the target immediately after the bombs had been dropped, shows an enormous crater beside No. 9 with smoke still hanging over this hangar, and the east side of the roof completely discoloured. A considerable volume of smoke proceeding from No. 4 is also shown, confirming the observers' reports of a burst between that and No. 3, which was reported as having set fire to both.

During these raids there was no interference from hostile aeroplanes, and anti-aircraft fire was negligible, so that the observations of effects by those taking part in the raids could be carefully made and noted without interruption. From a careful study of observers' reports and photographs it appears certain that at least one hostile single-seater was destroyed on the ground, one aeroplane shed demolished by a direct hit, a second completely destroyed by fire, and two others seriously damaged and probably burnt.

On September 3, Morhange Aerodrome was detailed as the objective for the combined bombing operations. The weather was again favourable in the afternoon, with a west wind of 20-25 m.p.h. at 12,000 feet. Two formations, again led by Capt. Stevenson and Lieut. Marshall, left at 3.55 p.m., eleven machines completing the raid. The Squadron was still handicapped by the inability of inexperienced pilots to obtain the best results from the B.H.P. engine at bombing heights, three machines having dropped out of formation for this reason before crossing the Lines. The raid was again carried out without serious interference either from E.A. or A.A. fire, excellent results being obtained. Bombs were dropped from 12,500 feet, falling well grouped on the south-east corner of the aerodrome. Observers reported two hostile machines destroyed on the ground, two bursts within a few yards of hangars, and two on the railway line close behind the southern line of hangars. In all, thirteen heavy and eighteen 25 lb. Cooper's bombs were dropped. Photographs (99 D.A. 117 and 118) taken on the raid show what appear to be ten or eleven bursts from heavy bombs very closely grouped in front of two hangars and on the road in the south-east corner of the aerodrome, one on the railway line and a mass of smoke blowing across the railway and hangars to the south-west of the main group. There are a few small patches of smoke to be seen in the same neighbourhood, which, however, cannot be certainly identified as resulting from the Cooper bombs. The accuracy of sighting and grouping of the bombs on this raid were as good as ever obtained by the Squadron. Unfortunately there appears to have been no direct hit on a hangar, though the accuracy displayed was considerably greater than that of the previous day, when such excellent material effect was obtained at Buhl.

It is of interest to note that during these raids the method of bombing in formation attained its final form. The two formations of six machines flew so close together that bombs from all machines

Good Grouping on Morhange Aerodrome.

Morhange Aerodrome, 3/9/18.

SEPTEMBER 3RD

in the raid could be released simultaneously, there being no necessity for the leader of the second formation to sight the target independently. On approaching the objective, the leader manœuvred so as to pass over his target down wind. When about to release his bombs he signalled to his observer to fire a white Verey light. The remainder of the pilots in the formation released their bombs immediately they saw those of the leader leave his machine. The leader of the second formation similarly took his aim from that of the raid leader. On this day Capt. T. C. Creaghan reported for duty, and took over command of "C" Flight from Lieut. Marshall.

Second Lieut. S. Lane was struck off the strength on admission to Hospital, sick.

Lieuts. Marshall and Broadbent led formations on September 4th, which again attacked Morhange. Twelve machines crossed the Lines, but unfortunately the engine of Lieut. Brooks' machine was damaged by A.A. fire, and only eleven therefore completed the raid. Bombing was not quite up to the standard of the previous day, though the majority of bursts were observed on the southern and western portions of the aerodrome among trenches. One direct hit on a hangar, of the row alongside the railway, is shown on Photo. 99 D.A. 121.

Lieut. H. Sanders rejoined the Squadron from England, having recovered from his wound, received on June 27th.

The first of the 400 h.p. Liberty D.H. 9 A's, which were intended to replace the D.H. 9's, was flown for the first time in the Squadron. The engine ran very smoothly, and the machine, though heavier to handle than the D.H. 9, met with universal approval. From this date the senior pilots continued to practice on the few D.H. 9 A's, which were received before the Armistice.

Lieut. Stevenson was promoted Captain, to fill the vacancy caused by the illness of Capt. Thom whilst on leave.

On the next two days the weather was unfit for flying, with low clouds and rain.

Capt. Beecroft rejoined from leave.

The Squadron was under orders for a twelve-machine raid on

Ludwigshafen on the Rhine opposite Mannheim, in company with two six-machine formations of 104 Squadron. A conference of the formation leaders took place, at which it was decided, on Major Pattinson's suggestion, that the raid should be carried out at 10,000 feet. The reasons for this decision, contrary to the usual principle of flying as high as possible, were as follows :—Mannheim was 97 miles from the nearest point of the Lines, and it was therefore doubtful whether, with a strong wind, the petrol capacity of the D.H. 9 would be sufficient to complete the journey, if speed were reduced and length of time for climb and rendezvous increased by flying at maximum height. On such a long raid it was considered that any hostile machines wishing to engage the formations would, with their superior speed and climb, easily reach the D.H. 9's before the latter could recross the Lines. Previous experience had shown that at least 75 per cent. of the machines which had failed to keep with their formations had done so after reaching 10,000 feet; also that it was much easier to keep a large formation well together when the pilots were not compelled to fly with throttles fully open in order to maintain height. It was considered that as the formations were sure to be attacked, it was of the utmost importance that no risk should be taken of leaving machines behind, unable to climb to bombing height, or being delayed by stragglers suffering from defective altitude control whilst travelling to or from the objective.

The following observers reported for duty :—2nd Lieuts. C. Bridgett, J. W. Howard, C. B. Wogan-Browne, and J. Potter.

On September 6th, only limited practice flying could be undertaken.

A heavy ground mist completely covered Azelot and the surrounding country at dawn on September 7th. By 10 a.m. conditions were improving rapidly, and at 11 a.m. two six-machine formations, led by Major Pattinson and Capt. Stevenson, with two emergency machines, and accompanied by the same number of 104 Squadron, left the ground. Weather conditions were excellent, though the wind reading was somewhat unfavourable at 20-25 m.p.h. south-west at 10,000 feet. The meeting of the two formations of

"A Direct Hit," Morhange Aerodrome, 4/9/18.

104 Squadron Photograph of Bombing at Morhange Aerodrome, 4/9/18.

SEPTEMBER 7TH

99 Squadron was entirely satisfactory, these being well together at 10,000 feet over the aerodrome, forty minutes after leaving the ground. Unfortunately the usual difficulty arose in combining the two Squadrons, and after eighty minutes the raid leader, Major Pattinson, was compelled to cross the Lines with the formations of 104 Squadron more than a mile behind, and approximately 1000 feet above those of 99 Squadron. The justification of the limit height of 10,000 feet was at once apparent, as the twelve machines of 99 Squadron detailed for the raid crossed the Lines in formation, and the two emergency pilots were compelled to return to their aerodrome, not being required; after arriving at the Lines well above the formations and with their engines running satisfactorily. Shortly after crossing the Lines, six or more hostile machines attacked from behind, concentrating principally against the rear formations. The enemy continued to attack for a considerable distance, shooting down two machines of 104 Squadron and also wounding Lieut. Broadbent and disabling his machine. To the great loss of the Squadron this officer and his observer, Lieut. Dunn, were compelled to land and were taken prisoner. The enemy broke off the engagement when the formations of 104 Squadron had closed with those of 99. No further serious fighting occurred till the objective was reached, although a number of isolated scouts were in the air, and occasionally opened fire at long range. When approaching the objective from the east it was seen that both Mannheim and Ludwigshafen, including the Badische Anilin and Soda Fabric, which was the target detailed, were covered by a dense pall of smoke or fog, through which it was impossible to distinguish the target, till almost vertically above. At about 11,000 feet were circling some fifteen hostile scouts of various types. The leader decided that, in order to bomb the objective satisfactorily, it would be necessary to swing his formations on to their bombing course some considerable distance short of the target; slow up so as to close the formations as well as possible, and fly straight ahead till all bombs had been released. This plan was successfully carried out, machines being very close together over the objective, and not more than sixty yards separating the individual formations. The enemy

attacked the centre and rear machines of the raid from the south, several actually diving through between the formations. Whilst this fight was in progress the raid leader dropped his bombs, followed by all the other pilots. In the meanwhile one D.H. 9 of 104 Squadron had been shot down, and several E.A.'s were reported to have fallen to the guns of the observers of that Squadron. During the combat the pilots showed the greatest possible steadiness and no tendency to scatter. On seeing that all bombs had been released, the formations well together, and a group of six or eight hostile scouts preparing to renew the attack from the right flank, the leader risked a somewhat sudden turn so as to bring the pilots' guns on to the enemy. The turn was admirably executed, the whole raid wheeling into the new course without loss of cohesion. This manœuvre, with its threat of simultaneous attack from 19 D.H. 9's, decided the fight and scattered the hostile formation. On the return journey no concerted attack was made on the bombers, although a considerable exchange of fire took place between the formations and a number of isolated machines, mainly at long range. Soon after leaving Mannheim, one machine of 104 Squadron commenced to lose height and fly very slowing, owing to a partially disabled engine. This necessitated considerable slowing and loss of height for the whole raid-formation, most of the return journey being accomplished at 8000, and the Lines being recrossed at about 7000 feet. Owing to the indifferent visibility, the intensity of the combat over the objective, and the fact that photographs were completely spoiled by mist, bombing results were difficult to ascertain. Observers of 99 Squadron reported eight direct hits on the Soda Fabric.

The total time spent in the air by machines on this raid was four hours, of which two hours and twenty minutes were spent beyond the Lines. Twelve machines of 99 and ten of 104 Squadron crossed the Lines, of which eleven of 99 dropped bombs and returned safely. Seven machines of 104 Squadron recrossed the Lines. This was the Squadron's most successful raid as regards the distance over the Lines, the number of machines which reached the objective, and the lightness of the casualties.

SEPTEMBER 7TH

The arrangement of the two formations is given below, the Squadron identification letter or figure of each machine being shown:—

		6	Major Pattinson		
			Lieut. Taylor		
Y	Lieut. McKeever			3	Lieut. Sanders
	Lieut. Boniface				Lieut. Beale
		F	Capt. Creaghan		
			Lieut. Notley		
1	Lieut. Poulton			T	Lieut. Hunter
	Sergt. Lee		———		Lieut. Swann
		C	Capt. Stevenson		
			Lieut. Walker		
2	Lieut. Jones			K	Lieut. Marshall
	Lieut. Black				Lieut. Speed
		D	Lieut. Broadbent		
			Lieut. Dunn		
A	Lieut. Crosbie-Chopin			4	Lieut. Springett
	Lieut. Bower		———		Lieut. Barns

The following pilot and observer reported for duty :—2nd Lieuts. C. R. G. Abrahams and G. A. Shipton.

The weather was very unfavourable for flying on the next day, with a strong wind and very low clouds.

Capt. Creaghan unfortunately fell and broke his collar-bone, a most unlucky accident.

Owing to sickness the Squadron lost three more pilots, who were admitted to Hospital, Lieuts. Hodder, Irving and Warwick.

On September 9th, the weather was again bad, no flying being done. A telegram was received in the Squadron announcing the award of the Distinguished Flying Cross to Major Pattinson for his successful leadership on the raid to Ludwigshafen.

Lieut. Marshall was later also awarded the Distinguished Flying Cross for the sustained excellence of his work over the Lines, and in particular for the parts played by him in this raid and in the course of the attacks on hostile aerodromes at the beginning of the month.

Second Lieut. R. C. Hardy was transferred to the Home Establishment.

On Tuesday, the 10th, bad weather again stopped all flying. The preliminary bombardment for the American attack on the St. Mihiel salient could now be heard from Azelot.

The hopelessly bad weather continued over the 11th. General Trenchard personally congratulated the Squadron-Commander on the success of recent operations undertaken by 99 Squadron.

On the night of the 11-12th, orders were received to commence the bombing of Courcelles Railway Junction, east of Metz, 13 miles beyond the Lines, as early as possible on the next morning, in support of the attack on the Saint Mihiel salient. September 12th dawned most unfavourably, with very low clouds, strong wind, and rainstorms at frequent intervals. An attempt was made by two formations to carry out a raid at 7.50 a.m. during a time of slight improvement in the weather, but had to be abandoned owing to continuous low clouds and rain. After standing by for some hours in the hope of an improvement, which would render formation bombing possible, it was decided that machines should go out in pairs led by an experienced pilot, followed by one less experienced.

Capt. Stevenson with Lieut. Walker, and Lieut. Springett with Lieut. Barns, left accordingly at noon with two 112 lb. bombs each. Courcelles Junction was successfully attacked from 5000 feet, four 112 lb. bombs being dropped, of which two were seen to burst on the railway lines. Between 3 and 4 p.m. Capt. Beecroft and Lieut. Taylor, with Lieut. Gillett and Lieut. Crossley, followed shortly afterwards by Lieut. Marshall and Lieut. Speed, with Lieut. Crosbie-Chopin and Lieut. Bower, attempted to reach Courcelles, but were prevented by very low clouds and bad visibility. One 230 lb. and four 112 lb. bombs were dropped on Orny village, which was observed to be full of transport, one direct hit being observed. Two 112 lb. bombs were dropped on the sidings and station of Verny, results being unobserved. These objectives are S.S.E. from Metz, approximately eight miles from the Lines. Bombs were dropped from 3000 feet, from which height the ground could be occasionally seen through gaps in the lowest layer of clouds. During the raids carried out on this day, anti-aircraft fire was very heavy and accurate, but no hostile machines were seen.

Towards evening the weather became worse, no further operations being possible.

At dawn on the next day there were heavy cloud banks at 2000-3000 feet with a strong northerly wind. At 7 a.m. fourteen machines left the ground to bomb Metz Sablon between the clouds. Before crossing the Lines, continuous clouds were encountered between 5000 and 8000 feet. Capt. Beecroft, who was leading, decided to abandon the raid and descended through the clouds. The formations became broken whilst in the clouds. Lieuts. Sanders and Springett decided to cross the Lines on a compass course, came out of the clouds at about 200 feet, dropping their bombs on a village occupied by the enemy and on a railway siding near Verny. Owing to bad visibility and the fact that fifteen-second-delay fuses were fitted to the bombs it was impossible to observe the bursts. All the machines returned safely to Azelot after various adventures at a very low altitude amongst the hills round Nancy. As there was no likelihood of an early improvement in the weather, it was decided at 10.30 a.m. that individual pilots should attempt to reach Metz flying in rain at an average height of 500 feet. Accordingly Lieuts. Wood and Bridgett left at 11 a.m. These officers did not return, and it was ascertained from the local inhabitants, after the Armistice had been signed, that their machine was shot down after leaving Metz, and both killed. At noon, Lieuts. Ogilvie and Shipton also started. Owing to his difficulty in finding the way in rain, the pilot decided to bomb Ars Junction, a few miles south of Metz. Two 112 lb. bombs were dropped, one of which was observed to burst on the sidings. Anti-aircraft and machine-gun fire from the ground were very heavy. Lieut. Shipton was able to locate two machine-guns in the Moselle Valley, and silenced one with his two Lewis guns.

At 2.30 p.m. six machines left the ground together under slightly better weather conditions, manned by the following pilots and observers :—Capt. Beecroft and Lieut. Notley, Lieuts. Sanders and Beale, Lieut. Poulton and Sergt. Lee, Lieuts. Gillett and Crossley, Lieuts. Dick and Smith, and Lieuts. McKeever and Boniface. These flew up the valley of the Moselle, encountering very low clouds, which prevented their reaching Metz. Two 230 lb., four 112 lb., and eight 25 lb. bombs were dropped on Ars sidings and station from 1000 feet. From heavy bombs, four bursts were observed on the railway and two within a few yards of the slidings. Four 25 lb. bombs burst in the village, which was crowded with troops and transport. Two hundred rounds were fired at hostile troops on the roads. Lieut. McKeever obtained a direct hit with a 230 lb. bomb in a yard full of transport at Arnaville.

Capt. Stevenson and Lieut. Walker, with Lieuts. Springett and Barns, left the ground shortly after the raid mentioned above.

A large mechanical transport park was observed on the Verny-Cherisey road. Capt. Stevenson dropped two 112 lb. bombs, which burst in a hutted camp beside the park, and Lieut. Springett obtained a direct hit with a 230 lb. bomb among the transport vehicles. Two formations of hostile scouts were successfully evaded between the clouds. The eight machines which took part in these raids returned to their aerodrome in spite of very intense anti-aircraft and machine-gun fire. Lieut. Notley received a flesh wound in the leg from a piece of shell-case. At 4.30 p.m. a six-machine formation, led by Lieut. Marshall, set out for Metz. One machine was compelled to return before crossing the Lines with the engine vibrating badly. The remainder were heavily attacked by eight enemy aircraft over Arnaville Junction, where six 112 lb. and two 230 lb. bombs were dropped, results being unobserved owing to the combat and to the target being partly covered by clouds. In the course of the fighting the machine of Lieuts. Crosby and Wogan-Browne was unfortunately shot down, falling just south of Pont-a-Mousson. Both pilot and observer were killed. Lieut. Hunter was slightly wounded in the leg by a machine-gun bullet. One hostile machine was destroyed by Lieut. Black, flying with Lieut. Jones. Considering that the pilots and observers were unaccustomed to flying low over the Lines, the very bad weather conditions, and the fact that the Moselle Valley was always very heavily defended, the Squadron had good reason for satisfaction in a day's work, in which fifteen machines dropped bombs on important targets. 2nd Lieut. R. Henderson and Sergt. S. Berwick reported for duty as observers.

On the next day two high bomb-raids of the usual type were carried out on Metz Sablon and one on Buhl Aerodrome. Capt. Stevenson left the ground with a formation of six at 7.25 a.m. Unfortunately Lieut. Dick with a broken connecting rod in his engine, and Lieut. Springett, with misfiring trouble, were compelled to leave the formation before crossing the Lines. The remaining four machines were attacked before reaching Metz by 18-20 hostile machines. Capt. Stevenson, with his formation, nevertheless reached his objective, where bombs were dropped, results being unobserved owing to the intensity of the fighting. Lieuts. Ogilvie and Shipton were shot down near Metz, but landed safely and were taken prisoner. The remaining three machines returned to their aerodrome, after beating off the enemy. One hostile machine was driven down out of control by Sergt. Jones, flying with Capt. Stevenson, and another left the fight, obviously damaged, after being engaged by Lieut. Boniface with Lieut. McKeever. When over Metz, Lieut. Dennis was very severely wounded by a machine-gun bullet, which passed through his back and perforated his intestines in many places. With great determination he maintained his position in formation, brought his machine back 37 miles, and made an excellent landing. His condition was critical when he was admitted to the 8th Canadian Stationary Hospital at Charmes, but, thanks to the skilful treatment which he received there, he was reported as being " out of danger " within a few days. He was awarded the Distinguished Flying Cross by the G.O.C. Independent Force in recognition of the extraordinary courage and endurance shown by him in bringing back his machine intact. His observer, Lieut. Ramsay, was slightly wounded in the leg during the engagement.

The second raid of the day was led by Capt. Beecroft to Buhl Aerodrome, five machines reaching the objective out of the six which started. The overheating of Lieut. Poulton's machine prevented his keeping up with the formation. One direct hit on the third hangar south of the largest one, and another very near the north end of the latter, were reported by observers. The photographs taken on this raid unfortunately did not include the majority of the bursts.

At 3.50 p.m. thirteen machines, led by Capts. Beecroft and Stevenson, left the ground for a second raid on Metz. Of these, Lieuts. Sanders, Bowyer, and Dick dropped out of formation with engine trouble. The remaining ten pilots dropped their bombs on the target detailed, excellent results being reported. Six direct hits on the Triangle, one on the railway near the Goods Station, and two on the Railway Works west of the Triangle, were observed. A photograph (99 D.A. 148) shows a considerable volume of smoke, apparently indicating several bursts on and beside the railway on the east side of the Triangle, one burst on the sidings to the south, and two others clear of the objective to the south-east. No hostile machines were encountered, though 35 were counted on the ground at Frescati Aerodrome, south of Metz.

Capt. P. E. Welchman, M.C., D.F.C., joined from No. 55 Squadron to command "C" Flight in place of Capt. Creaghan.

Lieut. J. K. Speed was struck off the strength on admission to Hospital, sick.

The following officers reported for duty :—Lieut. C. E. W. Thresher and 2nd Lieut. L. V. Russell as pilots. 2nd Lieuts. F. O. Cook and W. Glew as observers.

On the next day the Squadron was again detailed to bomb Metz, with two formations of 104 Squadron. Twelve bombers and two emergency machines left at 9.45 a.m., led by Capt. Welchman and Lieut. Sanders. The twelve machines originally detailed, and one emergency machine reached the objective, excellent results being obtained. Four bursts were reported among the locomotive sheds, three on the railway lines in the Triangle, and four just clear of the objective to the east. The majority of these bursts were confirmed by photographs. At this time the efficiency and morale of the Squadron were excellent. In spite of the heavy casualties of the previous days and the great damage to machines owing to fire from the ground, fourteen machines out of the establishment of eighteen were found fit to cross the Lines on a raid, and in the afternoon four left the ground for test and practice flying. In spite

Railway Triangle at Metz-Sablon with smoke from Bombs.

DE HAVILAND 9A.

SEPTEMBER 15TH

of the comparative inexperience of most of the pilots concerned, the grouping of the bombs which were dropped in heavy anti-aircraft fire was very good, showing steadiness under fire and confidence in the formation leaders.

A climbing test was carried out on the D.H. 9 A, which gave an interesting comparison between the performance of that machine and of the D.H. 9. The results of this test were as follows, normal performance of a B.H.P., D.H. 9 being given for comparison :—

	D.H. 9 A.	D.H. 9.
Load of bombs..	Two 230 lb.	One 230 lb.
Height after 47 min. ..	15,000 feet	12,000 feet
Height after 62 min. ..	16,000 feet	13,500 feet
Height after 70 min. ..	16,500 feet	14,000 feet

Capt. Beecroft and Lieuts. Walker and Taylor were admitted to Hospital sick, and finally transferred to the Home Establishment. These officers had all been unwell for several weeks, but had continued their flying duties, and avoided the Medical Officer, till the younger pilots and observers had been trained to take their places. As three of the original members, who had played a great part in forming the Squadron tradition, their loss was a heavy one.

Lieut. Sanders was promoted Captain, to command "B" Flight, in place of Capt. Beecroft.

On September 16th, Capt. Welchman led his second raid for 99 Squadron, followed by Lieut. Sanders, leading the second formation. Of the fourteen machines which left the ground, twelve crossed the Lines, one pilot being compelled to return later owing to the sickness of his observer. Finding the wind approximately 35 m.p.h. south, the leader decided to bomb Hagenau Aerodrome instead of proceeding to Karlsruhe, the original objective. Unfortunately a Squadron record was spoilt by the only failure of a heavy bomb to leave the machine when over the objective. Twelve 112 lb. and four 230 lb. bombs were dropped. Observers reported excellent grouping about the hangars in the N.W. corner of the Aerodrome ; two direct hits on large sheds in the line running E.N.E. and W.S.W., one of which was set on fire, three burst a few yards in front of these sheds, one of which was within five yards of a machine on the ground ; one direct hit on a shed in the line running E.S.E., and one on smaller buildings just behind the aeroplane sheds. A photograph (99 D.A. 161) confirms one direct hit on the end of a large shed, which has apparently caused a fire ; four or five bursts on the aerodrome between twenty and one hundred yards from the sheds, two of which have narrowly missed an aeroplane, and two more aeroplanes within fifty yards of exploding bombs. As regards accuracy of sighting and closeness of grouping this raid was one of the best ever carried out by No. 99 Squadron.

Lieuts. C. C. Gilbert and 2nd Lieuts. G. M. Power, V. J. Fontannaz, and C. M. Sharp reported for duty.

Owing to unfavourable weather with very low clouds and strong wind, no operations were carried out from September 17th-24th inclusive, only a limited amount of practice-flying being possible.

A test climb on a D.H. 9 A., fitted with three 112 lb. bombs, gave excellent results. A height of 15,000 feet was reached in 42 minutes, and 17,000 in 62 minutes. Actual air speed at the latter height was found to be 87 miles per hour. Practice flying was continued both with D.H. 9's and D.H. 9 A.'s. Major Pattinson took command of the 41st Wing in the absence of Lieut.-Colonel Baldwin on leave. The former did not rejoin the Squadron, being promoted to command the Wing on his return from leave on October 19th, to fill the vacancy caused by Colonel Baldwin's transfer to the Home Establishment. The following officers joined the Squadron :— As pilots—Lieut. H. S. H. Read, 2nd Lieuts. V. C. Varcoe and E. C. Brown. As observers—2nd Lieuts. W. J. Tremellen and R. E. Fox. Owing to sickness the following observers were admitted to Hospital and struck off the strength :—2nd Lieuts. R. Henderson and J. Potter.

On September 25th, a very unsuccessful attempt was made to bomb an objective near Rastatt. Unfortunately Lieut. Marshall, who was leading one formation, was compelled to return before crossing the Lines with engine trouble, and the remainder of his formation became confused and returned individually to the aerodrome. Capt. Sanders, with the five remaining machines, bombed

"A Good Shot," Hagenau Aerodrome.

SEPTEMBER 25TH

Buhl Aerodrome. No direct hits were observed. Lieut. Oliphant was slightly wounded. The failure of this raid showed the weakness of the Squadron with regard to experienced pilots. At this time it was difficult to continue operations with D.H. 9's, as there were only twelve of these on the Squadron's strength, and six D.H. 9 A.'s. It was impracticable to use the two types on a raid, and experience had proved that at least fifteen machines were necessary in order to produce daily twelve capable of crossing the Lines.

Second Lieut. C. B. Fairhurst joined the Squadron for duty as observer.

Second Lieut. M. J. Poulton was admitted to Hospital, and struck off the strength, having injured himself in crashing his machine.

Only ten D.H. 9's were serviceable on the 26th, when a raid on Thionville was ordered at short notice, in connection with operations on the ground. This raid was most disastrous. The engine on Capt. Sanders' machine broke a connecting rod, and Lieut. Dick returned before crossing the Lines owing to trouble with the altitude control on his engine. The remaining pilots of "B" Flight's formation, with the exception of Lieut. King, who could not get into position, joined with the other formation led by Capt. Welchman, which thus crossed the Lines with seven machines. For the second time in the Squadron's history the Germans attacked successfully with overwhelming odds on their side. Before reaching Metz, approximately thirty hostile scouts in two formations were encountered. Capt. Welchman perceived that it would be quite impossible to reach Thionville, and gave the signal for bombs to be dropped on Metz Sablon. The fighting was very intense and the range short. Of the seven D.H. 9's which crossed the Lines, only one, piloted by Lieut. West, actually returned to Azelot, carrying the body of the observer, Lieut. Howard, who had been killed by a machine-gun bullet. Lieut. McKeever's machine was almost completely destroyed by bullets, but the pilot, although wounded in the foot, managed to land successfully near Pont-a-Mousson with his observer, Lieut. Boniface, unhurt. Out of the personnel of the five machines which were brought down in German territory, Capt.

Welchman was very severely wounded in the lungs, and died of his wounds in Charmes Hospital, having been removed from the Lazarette Saint Clement at Metz shortly after the Armistice. His observer, Lieut. Swann, was brought back at the same time suffering from a severe wound in the leg. Lieuts. Gilbert and Buckby, Abrahams and Sharp, and Stern and Cook, were all killed in action. Lieuts. Gillett and Crossley were taken prisoners, the latter being slightly wounded.

The intensity of the combat rendered complete and accurate observation of bombing and fighting results impossible. Survivors' reports agreed, however, that the enemy lost at least one machine in flames, one which collapsed in the air, and two out of control.

As a result of the losses on September 26th, only three D.H. 9's were serviceable on the following day, and the shortage of experienced pilots was rendered more acute. The weather was unfavourable for operations up till September 30th inclusive, and only a moderate amount of practice flying on D.H. 9's and D.H. 9 A.'s could be undertaken.

To the satisfaction of all concerned, Capt. Thom rejoined the Squadron on recovering from influenza, and took command from September 27th.

Lieut. West left the Squadron on transfer to the Home Establishment for a change of duty.

From September 27th-30th inclusive, the following changes in personnel occurred :—Lieuts. Shaw and Henderson rejoined from Hospital ; 2nd Lieut. D. C. Bain joined for duty as pilot, and 2nd Lieut. P. James and Sergt. P. A. Cuka as observers. The weather was unfit for operations, although a certain amount of practice-flying was done.

Practice-flying with both D.H. 9's and D.H. 9 A.'s was continued from October 1st to 6th, the Squadron being reinforced in numbers of the former type, though again disappointed as regards the latter. An average of 19 hours flying per day was carried out during this time.

On the next two days the weather proved unfit for flying.

General Trenchard visited the Squadron and stimulated the pilots and observers to further efforts ; and on the 9th, a successful raid, led by Capts. Stevenson and Sanders, was carried out, eleven machines dropping bombs on Metz Sablon. Four bursts were observed in the Railway Triangle. Anti-aircraft fire was unusually heavy and accurate on this raid, and considerable damage was done, although all machines safely regained the aerodrome.

On October 11th, Capt. Thom and Capt. Stevenson led formations to Metz, where excellent results were obtained, five direct hits in the Triangle, two on a factory to the south-east, and one on the Barracks to the south-west. The majority of the bursts were confirmed by photographs.

From October 12th-17th inclusive, the weather prevented operations from being carried out, and little practice-flying was possible.

On the 18th, Capts. Stevenson and Sanders led the first of three more raids on Metz Sablon. Visibility was very poor, but in spite of the difficulty of using bomb-sights, several bursts on the objective were observed.

After two more days of bad weather, the second raid was carried out under the leadership of Capt. Sanders. Observation was impossible owing to clouds and haze.

On the 23rd, Capt. Thom with Capt. Stevenson, led the third raid on Metz. Shortly after the bombs had been dropped, fourteen hostile machines attacked, but were successfully driven away, one being shot down out of control by Lieut. Burrows, flying with Lieut. Hodder. Lieut. Collis was severely wounded in the legs, but successfully landed his machine on a French aerodrome near Nancy.

On October 24th, 25th and 26th, bad weather stopped all flying.

On the following day, Frescaty Aerodrome was bombed by formations led by Capt. Thom and Capt. Sanders. Ten D.H. 9's reached the objective, which was almost completely obscured by clouds. Several bursts were observed in the centre of the aerodrome.

Morhange Aerodrome was revisited on the next day ; eleven machines, under the leadership of Capts. Stevenson and Sanders, reaching the objective. Satisfactory results were reported :—One direct hit on a hangar, one burst on the southern portion of the aerodrome, and four on the sidings to the south-east. Capt. Thom, flying at about 15,000 feet on a D.H. 9 A., dropped three 112 lb. bombs on Frescaty, obtaining a direct hit on a hangar in the wood alongside the aerodrome. Two hostile scouts, which attempted to attack, were unable to reach the D.H. 9 A.

On October 29th, the railways at Longuyon were attacked. Capts. Thom and Sanders, with eleven machines, reached the objective. Seven 230 lb. and eight 112 lb. bombs were dropped, bursts being unobserved, owing to clouds and haze.

On the two succeeding days, Capt. Sanders led raids to Buhl Aerodrome.

On the first of these, his observer, Lieut. Power, shot down one of eight hostile machines which attacked near the objective and were successfully repulsed without inflicting any losses on the bombers.

On the second raid one hangar received a direct hit.

Capt. H.R.H. Prince Albert, K.G., and Major Greig arrived at the Squadron for a visit of ten days under active service conditions.

This event stimulated the social life of Azelot to a considerable extent, and resulted in a plethora of " guest nights " and visits to Nancy during a time when bombing activity was limited by bad weather. The visitors' habit of taking running exercise, suitably dressed, excited no little interest by its novelty in the lethargic community of pilots and observers ; but it is not recorded that the example was largely followed.

No operations were carried out on November 1st, but, in spite of very low clouds and bad visibility on the next day, Capt. Sanders carried out an individual raid on Avrincourt Junction, about seven miles from the Lines, dropping three 112 lb. bombs from 2000 feet. A direct hit was obtained on an ammunition dump, where a considerable explosion was caused.

On the 3rd, Capt. Thom and Capt. Stevenson reached Buhl Aerodrome with eleven machines, in spite of thick clouds. Through a gap in the clouds three bursts were observed alongside the largest shed, and three more on the aerodrome close to the hangars.

Bad weather stopped service flying on the 4th.

SEPTEMBER 27TH

On this day, Major C. R. Cox, A.F.C., arrived and took over command of the Squadron from Capt. Thom.

After an unsuccessful attempt on the 5th, Buhl was again attacked on the 6th.

Ten machines bombed the objective, and several bursts were observed in the vicinity of the hangars.

The formation was attacked by twenty hostile scouts, and one D.H. 9 was shot down under control. Lieut. Bower with Lieut. Crosbie-Choppin shot down one hostile machine, which was seen to crash ; a second went down in flames after being engaged by Lieut. Burrows flying with Lieut. Warwick, and a third was disabled by Lieut. Llewellen with Lieut. King, and went down emitting a considerable volume of dense smoke.

During the 7th and 8th, only a little practice-flying was possible, owing to misty weather and low clouds.

On November 9th, low clouds again rendered formation flying impossible, but three pilots attempted individual raids at about 500 feet on D.H. 9 A.'s.

Capt. Thom and Lieut. Duggan succeeded in reaching railway objectives within eighteen miles of the Lines, on which two 230 lb. and three 112 lb. bombs were dropped. Major Cox was unable to find his way over country which was new to him, and in conditions of great difficulty, and landed at Toul Aerodrome without having released his bombs.

On the next day an uneventful raid on Morhange Aerodrome was executed under the leadership of Capt. Stevenson and Major Cox ; and on that evening the long-awaited instructions were received that the twelve D.H. 9 A.'s, still needed fully to refit the Squadron, were to be collected.

The fact that these machines had not been received in time to carry out a long raid, provided the only regret with which the majority of No. 99 Squadron received the joyous news of the signature of the Armistice on November 11th.

Those members of the Independent Force who had not seen the defeat of the German Army, and to whom no appreciable weakening of the enemy's forces had been apparent, heard of the overwhelming nature of the Armistice terms with boundless delight, not unmixed with surprise.

This history, which commenced with the preparation of the Squadron for active service, will here end at the period when, with the commencement of demobilisation, its members were scattered and removed to other spheres of activity.

It is necessary to mention the very serious epidemic of influenza, which occurred in the winter of 1918-19, and caused the deaths of both the Squadron's Warrant Officers, Sergeant-Majors Deeley and Martin, besides those of several members of the original " 99." These losses were most deeply felt by those who had been with the Squadron long enough to appreciate the hard times through which they had cheerfully carried out their difficult work.

> "Let us now praise famous men
> Men of little showing,
> For their work continueth,
> And their work continueth,
> Broad and deep continueth,
> Greater than their knowing."
>
> *(Rudyard Kipling.)*

INDEPENDENT FORCE
AREA OPERATIONS

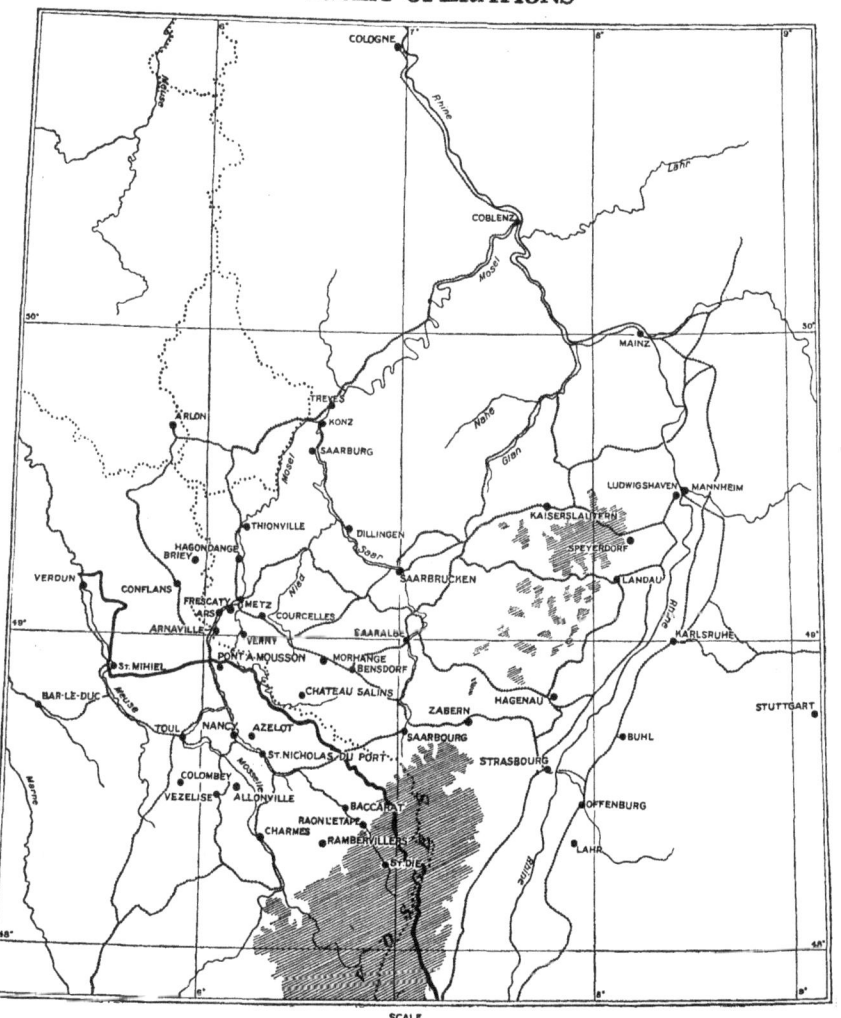

SUPPLEMENT "A."
HONOURS AND AWARDS.

The following immediate awards to members of 99 Squadron were gazetted between May 20th, 1918, the day on which the first operation was carried out, and the signing of the Armistice on November 11th :—

Extract from the *London Gazette*, August 3rd, 1918 :—

Awarded the Distinguished Flying Cross—
    Lieut. (Temp. Capt.) William Dorian Thom.

"A gallant and capable leader in long-distance bombing raids, in eighteen of which he has taken part during a period of six weeks. During the last raid his formation was attacked by thirteen enemy machines, but he nevertheless managed to drop his bombs on his objective, direct hits being obtained, and he also succeeded in destroying an enemy aeroplane."

Extract from the *London Gazette*, September 21st, 1918 :—

Awarded the Distinguished Flying Cross—
    Lieut. Marthinus Theunis Steyn Papenfus.

"This officer displayed excellent judgment in a recent raid. Keeping his formation well together and descending to a low altitude, he led them well over an enemy factory, and so enabled them to use their bombs most effectively. The success of this operation was largely due to his fine leadership. In addition, he has taken part in eighteen raids as deputy leader of the formation, invariably showing the greatest keenness and devotion to duty."

Lieut. William Beresford Walker—(HIGHLAND LIGHT INFANTRY).

"This officer has taken part in twenty-one bombing raids, and has rendered excellent and valuable service in photography and general observation. He has shown himself a brave and skilful officer in action, notably on one occasion, when his formation was attacked by twelve hostile scouts, which approached to within short range; he engaged one at 150 yards, and drove it down in flames. In another engagement he attacked one enemy aeroplane at close range and drove it down; he then engaged several others with good effect."

Awarded the Distinguished Flying Medal—
7054 Sergt.-Observer Frederick Lee (Ockley).

" During a recent long-distance bombing raid the formation to which Sergt. Lee belonged was attacked when over the objective by 20 enemy scouts. He engaged one of them with his double gun, which caused the enemy to turn over on his back, and after various gyrations the pilot fell out of the aeroplane. This N.C.O. has proved himself a gallant and skilful observer, and in all respects a most reliable man in the air."

Extract from the *London Gazette*, November 2nd, 1918 :—
Awarded the Distinguished Flying Cross—
2nd Lieut. James Gordon Dennis.

" On a recent bombing raid this officer was engaged in a formation which was attacked by twenty of the enemy, and in the ensuing fight he was severely wounded. He at once signalled to his observer to take charge of the machine, but the observer had also been wounded, and was unable to comply. Lieut. Dennis decided that his duty demanded that he should remain with his formation to the end of the battle, and this he did, notwithstanding the loss of blood from his wounds. He succeeded in bringing his machine back to our Lines—a distance of over forty miles—a feat which surprised his Commanding Officer."

Lieut. Keith Douglas Marshall.

" A very skilful, gallant, and determined air fighter, who has been engaged in twenty-seven successful bombing operations since 1st of May, 1918. Lieut. Marshall was the leader of a formation recently detailed to attack an enemy aerodrome, which resulted in the destruction of three enemy machines and eight hangars; no casualties were sustained by his party. This officer was engaged a few days later in a combined attack on a great enemy war factory. Just as the bombs were falling an enemy formation of fifteen machines appeared, and Lieut. Marshall turned quickly in their direction, which disconcerted the enemy so completely that they at once scattered and were unable to reform. During the progress of this bombing expedition thirty-two enemy machines were encountered."

Major Lawrence Arthur Pattinson, M.C. (ROYAL FUSILIERS).

" This officer is not only a capable and most efficient Squadron Commander, but also an exceptionally fine leader of bombing formations. On the 7th of September he led a combined formation of twenty-two machines; they were attacked by some thirty aircraft, who made the most determined effort to prevent our formation reaching their objective. By skilful leadership and manœuvring Major Pattinson repulsed the attack and dispersed the enemy formation. Leading well over the target, excellent results were obtained."

(M.C. gazetted June 3rd, 1916.)

Lieut. (Temp. Capt.) William Gordon Stevenson.

" A fine leader, who has taken part in twenty-six successful raids, displaying marked skill and gallantry, notably on the 7th of July, when, with five other machines, he carried out a successful raid. On the return journey the formation was engaged by ten hostile aircraft, who made repeated and determined attacks; that these attacks were repulsed without loss was largely due to the cool judgment and strong initiative shown by this officer."

2nd Lieut. Bryan Samuel William Taylor.

" A gallant and skilful observer, who has been engaged in nineteen successful bombing raids during the past five months. During one of these raids eight of our machines were attacked by twenty enemy aircraft on the return journey, and during the course of the close fighting (which had become somewhat confused), Lieut. Taylor destroyed an enemy aeroplane just at the moment when matters were critical for our formation, which resulted in affairs being straightened out immediately to our advantage. Lieut. Taylor has always distinguished himself by the efficient manner in which he has carried out any operation allotted him, notably the various long distance raids."

Extract from the Supplement to the *London Gazette*, January 1st, 1919 :—

Awarded the Meritorious Service Medal.
252 Chief Master Mechanic D. Martin, M.M.

Mentioned in Despatches.
Lieut. (A./Capt.) V. Beecroft.
2nd Lieut. O. Bell.
Major L. A. Pattinson, M.C., D.F.C.
Lieut. (A./Capt.) A. D. Taylor.
21352 Chief Mechanic A. E. Bott.

Extract from the Supplement to the *London Gazette*, June 4th, 1919. Honours for various Theatres of War :—

Distinguished Service Order.
Major (A./Lieut.-Colonel) L. A. Pattinson, M.C., D.F.C.

Bar to the Distinguished Flying Cross.
Capt. W. D. Thom, D.F.C.

Distinguished Flying Cross.
Lieut. (A./Capt.) V. Beecroft.

Distinguished Flying Medal.
402734 Sergt.-Mechanic J. Jones (Tonbury, Worcs.)

Mentioned in Despatches.
252 Sergt.-Major (1st) D. Martin, M.M.

SUPPLEMENT "B."

Extracts from the 10th Supplement to the *London Gazette*, December 31st, 1918.

Despatches from Sir H. M. Trenchard, Commanding the Independent Force, R.A.F. :—

"On the 31st of July, 99 Squadron, under the command of Capt. Taylor, went out to attack Mainz. They encountered forty hostile scouts south of Saarbrucken. Fierce fighting ensued, as a result of which four of our machines were shot down. The remaining five machines of the formation reached Saabrucken, and dropped their bombs on the Station. On their way home they were again attacked by large numbers of hostile scouts, and suffered the loss of three more of their number."

"On the 7th of September, eleven machines of 99 Squadron, followed by ten machines of 104 Squadron, made an almost simultaneous attack on Mannheim, where bombs were dropped with excellent results on the Badische Anilin and Soda Fabric. 99 Squadron obtained at least eight direct hits on the factory, but the results of 104 Squadron could not be observed owing to the mist and smoke. Both Squadrons were attacked on the outward and return journey and over the objective by superior numbers of hostile aircraft. The formation of 99 Squadron was led by Colonel (then Major) L. A. Pattinson, and the formation of 104 Squadron by Capt. R. J. Gammon.

"99 Squadron was attacked by six hostile machines fifteen miles over the Lines. These were driven off. Ten hostile machines attacked about fifteen miles over the Lines. They were also driven off. Fifteen hostile machines then attacked over the objective. After dropping bombs the formation turned towards the hostile machines, which apparently disconcerted them, as they became scattered. On the return journey several enemy scouts kept up a running fight, one scout attacking from in front was driven off by the leader's observer firing over the top plane. Over two tons of bombs were dropped at Mannheim in this raid."

NOTE 1.

Explanation of Terms and Abbreviations.

ALDIS SIGHT.—A form of self-aligning telescopic sight used by the pilot on a tractor machine. The sight was fixed in front of the pilot in alignment with the fixed Vickers gun, which fired in the line of flight of the machine and was controlled so as to fire between the revolving blades of the propeller.

B.H.P. ENGINE.—A six cylinder water-cooled engine made originally by the Beardmore firm, fitted to the D.H. 9 machine, giving about 230 h.p. The type fitted to the machines of No. 99 Squadron was a modified B.H.P., made by the Siddeley Company, and re-named the " Siddeley Puma."

BOMB RACKS.—Metal frames, made to carry one heavy bomb or four light bombs each, from which the bombs are suspended by hooks, which could be disengaged from the lugs on the bombs by means of a wire connected to a handle in the pilot's seat.

BOMB SIGHT.—On the machines used by 99 Squadron this consisted of a negative lens inserted in a hole in the floor of the pilot's cockpit and fitted with adjustable crossed-wires for direction and forward angle of aim. On looking through the lens the pilot would see in miniature a considerable tract of country below the machine and sight the bomb target by flying his machine so as to bring the intersection of the crossed-wires on to the point to be bombed. It was necessary to approach the target either immediately up or down wind, and it was found most convenient to use the latter method, so as to pass more quickly over the anti-aircraft guns, when flying in a straight line preparatory to bombing.

BOMB TARGET.—The point to be bombed was usually detailed in operation orders for the day. Targets of military importance were alone to be bombed. These included munition factories, railways, hostile aerodromes, etc. From August onwards, leaders of formations and individual pilots when alone ; if unable to reach any of the alternative objectives detailed, were allowed to bomb

EXPLANATION OF TERMS, Etc.

any targets of military importance in Germany proper, and certain railway targets and hostile aerodromes in Alsace Lorraine.

COOPER BOMB.—A type of 25 lb. bomb with instantaneous fuse with little power of penetration, but very great effect when used against targets in the open. Fragments from this bomb flew horizontally at a few feet above the ground instead of burying themselves in the earth, as in the case of a bomb designed to penetrate before exploding.

112 lb. BOMB.—This bomb was designed with a thick case so that it should penetrate before exploding and produce great effect on such targets as buildings, rolling stock, etc.

230 lb. BOMB.—As in the case of the 112 lb. bomb, considerable penetration was desired, but a thinner case was fitted so that more explosive was carried in proportion to the total weight. These two types could be fitted with instantaneous fuses to explode the bomb immediately on striking, $2\frac{1}{2}$ second delay fuses used when it was desired that the explosion should not occur till penetration had taken place, and 15 second delay fuses designed for use on machines when flying low over a target so as to give the pilot time to escape without the risk of being hit by his own bomb.

DELAY-ACTION FUSE.—This type was fitted to heavy bombs. On striking the ground a percussion cap was pierced by a firing pin and ignited a piece of slow-burning material which burnt for the required number of seconds before causing the bomb to explode.

D.H. 9.—The De Haviland No. 9 machine produced by the Aircraft Manufacturing Co., Ltd., was used by 99 Squadron. Engine, 230 h.p. Siddeley " Puma " B.H.P. The machine was a two-seated tractor biplane, with stream-lined front, and radiator placed behind the engine, and arranged so that the pilot could lower it on guides to project below the machine or withdraw it into the fuselage so as to keep the engine warm at high altitudes or on cold days.

The machine was very stable, and the tail plane could be set for climbing or gliding by means of a wheel control worked by the pilot.

An altitude control was fitted by means of which the pilot could produce suction in the float chamber of the carburettor, through a connection with the induction pipe, and thus reduce the supply of petrol to the carburettor jet.

Owing to the rarity of the atmosphere at altitudes of over 10,000 feet, engines tended to obtain too much petrol in proportion to the oxygen in the atmosphere, and it was therefore necessary to provide a device which would regulate the proportions.

On the D.H. 9 the petrol tanks were situated between the engine and the pilot's seat, which was immediately in front of that of the observer.

A Vickers gun firing in the line of flight and supplied by a belt of 250 rounds was provided for the pilot. The observer's armament consisted of two Lewis guns mounted parallel and rigidly attached to one another. The whole fitting was mounted so as to give an all-round fire.

Ten drums of ammunition, holding 97 rounds each, were carried in pigeon holes arranged round the observer's cockpit. The petrol and oil supplies carried were sufficient for about $5\frac{3}{4}$ hours flying, but varied considerably according to the running of individual engines.

Bombs carried were one 230 lb., two 112 lb., or eight to twelve 25 lb.

D.H. 9 A.—This machine was an improved type of D.H. 9. The principal points of difference were as follows :—400 h.p. 12 cylinder Liberty engine ; larger planes than those fitted to the D.H. 9 ; radiator in front of the engine instead of behind and below ; load carried, two 230 lb., or three 112 lb. bombs ; much superior speed and climb ; petrol and oil capacity for about $6\frac{1}{2}$ hours flying.

ENEMY AIRCRAFT " DESTROYED," " OUT OF CONTROL."—A hostile machine was considered to have been " destroyed " and the personnel killed if :

1. It was seen to have broken some large plane or fallen to pieces in the air.
2. It fell in flames.
3. It was seen to fall or dive down steeply and reach the ground in this manner.

EXPLANATION OF TERMS, ETC.

4. The pilot was seen to have fallen out at a considerable height. A machine was counted as " out of control " if it was seen to fall in such a manner and for such a distance that the pilot could be assumed to be incapable of bringing it to the ground in safety. In deciding whether a machine should be considered " out of control," great care was exercised not to claim such machines as performed some extraordinary manœuvre under circumstances in which it would have been to the pilot's advantage to do something surprising in order to escape from a difficult situation.

FORMATION FLYING.—Flying in a definite order in which each machine held a special position relative to the leader. The object of formation flying in a bombing squadron was to bring as many guns as possible to bear on an enemy at as nearly equal ranges as possible.

" GERMANY," OR " GERMANY PROPER."—This term excludes Alsace Lorraine, in which bomb-dropping was very much restricted, as it was always considered that these provinces belonged to France, and would be retaken in the event of victory. The nearest bomb target in " Germany Proper " was some forty miles from the trench line.

LIBERTY ENGINE.—A twelve cylinder 400 h.p. American-made engine, fitted in the D.H. 9 A.

SCOUT.—A single-seated machine used for fighting only. The German scouts were fitted with six cylinder water-cooled engines of 160 to 200 h.p. They carried two guns firing forward in the line of flight, with belts, which usually held about five hundred rounds of ammunition.

SIDDELEY " PUMA " ENGINE.—See note on B.H.P. engine.

" SPIN."—An aeroplane is said to spin when it falls in a nearly vertical dive, at the same time rotating approximately about its longitudinal axis.

The pilot may purposely put his machine into a spin for one or two thousand feet in order to escape from a difficult situation during a fight. As an aeroplane is likely to spin if the pilot is incapacitated, it was usually considered that for a machine to fall in this way for more than three or four thousand feet, when not engaged, was a sign of its being out of control.

FLIGHT, SQUADRON, WING, BRIGADE.—A flight was a Captain's command, and consisted of six bombing machines, six pilots, four to six observers, and about twenty mechanics. There were three aeroplane flights and a headquarter flight in a squadron. The Headquarters flight varied in different squadrons. In 99 Squadron it consisted of the transport vehicles and drivers; all mechanics who worked in headquarter workshops, such as carpenters, coppersmiths, instrument repairers, turners, etc., supervised by the Chief Master Mechanic or Technical Sergeant-Major, clerks and storemen under the Disciplinary Sergeant-Major, who was also responsible for the general administration of the camp and supervision of parades.

Headquarter flight officers were the Squadron Commander, Equipment Officer, Armament Officer and Recording Officer, and any spare pilots and observers who had not been definitely allotted to other flights.

A Wing consisted of an indefinite number of squadrons, usually three to seven. A Wing was commanded by a Lieutenant-Colonel, and had separate headquarters, which lived apart from the squadrons. Wing headquarters for bombing purposes consisted of a Wing Commander, an Adjutant, Equipment Officer, Photographic Officer, Intelligence Officer, Medical Officer, and sometimes a Navigation Officer.

A Brigade consisted of two or more Wings and an aircraft park for supplies. The staff resembled that of a Wing in most respects.

SCARFE MOUNTING.—This was the type of mounting used for carrying the observer's guns on the de Havilland machines. The base of the mounting consisted of a circular rail, round which revolved a ring on to which was hinged an arm, roughly semicircular in shape, which carried the socket for the clamp ring or forked bracket, which held the Lewis gun or guns. By means of a single clamping lever the height to which it was desired to swing the gun and the angle of the mounting relative to the line of flight could be fixed. When the mounting was unclamped the gun could be swung and elevated into any required position with great ease and quickness.

NOTE 2.

FORMATION FLYING.

The object of formation flying in a day-bombing squadron was to prevent the enemy from making a concerted attack on one or two machines at a time, and thus wipe out a bomb raid in a series of isolated engagements with odds always in his favour. In formation flying with D.H. 9 machines, which possessed a forward-firing gun for the pilot and an all-round field of fire for the observer, only restricted by the impossibility of firing downwards and directly behind, the following were the main essentials :—

1. Mutual supporting fire ; that is to say, if one machine were closely engaged, several other machines should be in a position to engage the enemy at effective range. This necessitated the distances between any machine and the two nearest not being more than about 75 yards ; the shorter the better. If one machine were engaged from behind, and below, or in front and to the flank, so that neither pilot nor observer could engage the enemy without losing formation position, it was necessary that one or more of the other machines of the formation should be able to bring effective fire to bear on the enemy.

2. Machines should not fly directly behind one another, or the slip stream or wash from that in front would throw that behind out of position.

3. The pilot of one machine in front of the formation must act as leader, and on his machine the remainder must take position. Responsibility for course and tactics therefore devolves on the leader. There must be a deputy leader to take the place of the leader in case of the former's becoming a casualty. The deputy leader must be able at any time to lead the formation, and must therefore follow the course on his map and compass. With the exception of the leader and deputy-leader, the pilots and observers were frequently ignorant of the course followed. This was of little

importance, compared with that of keeping in correct formation, engaging the enemy as necessary, and dropping bombs when over the objective.

It was found necessary to have certain signals from the leader, which were given by means of coloured lights, to show when bombs were to be dropped, when the formation was to break up, to descend through clouds over its aerodrome, etc.

4. The formation must be arranged so that the personnel of all other machines could see the leader's, and the leader could see all other machines.

5. Machines must not fly vertically under one another for fear of being hit by bombs.

6. Formations must not be so large as to become unmanageable on turns.

7. The speed and rate of climb must be those of the worst machine, but in operations where high speed and quick climbing, are essential, the leader must not reduce speed sufficiently to allow the slowest machine to fly at under its highest speed or best rate of climb.

N.B.—All bombing operations in the Independent Force were, as far as possible, carried out at the greatest possible height attained in the shortest possible time, consistent with close formation flying and crossing the Lines within a reasonable time after leaving the ground. The leader's great difficulty was to make a satisfactory compromise between these conflicting desiderata.

The type of formation used by 99 Squadron, and based on that of 55 Squadron, is shown in plan in the accompanying diagram. (Figures show the heights of the other machines relative to the leader.)

The deputy-leader is immediately behind the leader. In order to keep close to his machine, it was necessary for the two machines flanking the leader to be a little above him, and very little behind, in order that their pilots should obtain an unrestricted view of him over their bottom planes. In the case of the pilots of the rear machines, the views of those in front was limited by top planes above and engines below. In order to maintain close touch with those in

FORMATION FLYING

front and to see them clearly it was necessary not to lose height, as by so doing the view was obstructed by the top plane. In very close formation flying the intervals shown in the diagram were frequently reduced. Formations were usually attacked from behind, and it was the duty of the deputy-leader to adjust his position so as to give his observer a good cross shot at any hostile machine attacking the right or left rear machine from the blind spot under its tail.

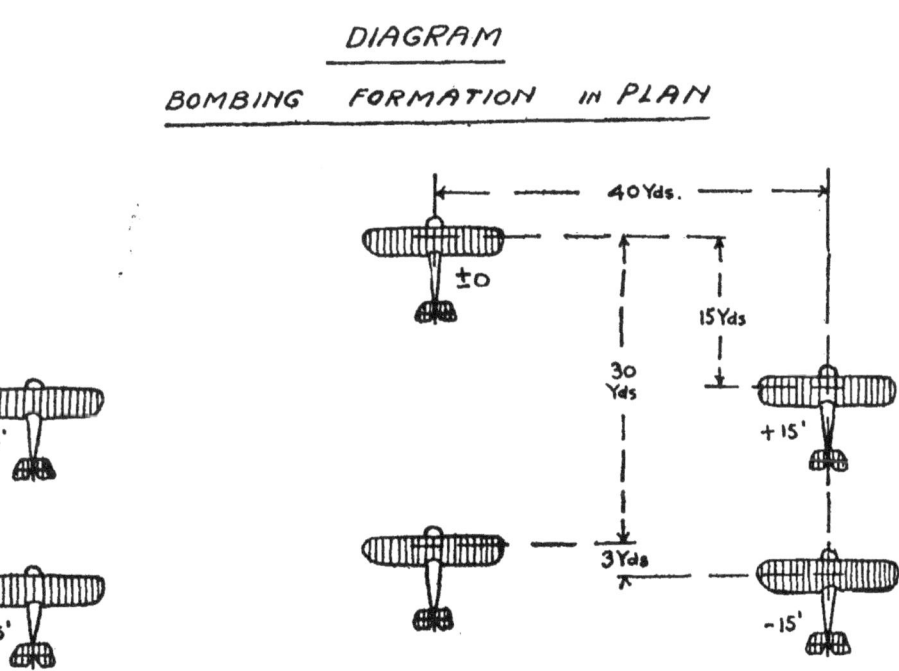

Figures + or − indicate differences in height, up or down

NOTE 3.
Summary of Work and Results
May 21st to November 10th, 1918, inclusive.

	May*	June	July	August	Sept.	Oct.	Nov.*	
Weight of bombs dropped	t. cwt. lb. 7 3 0	t. cwt. lb. 13 7 48	t. cwt. lb. 9 11 26	t. cwt. lb. 4 16 108	t. cwt. lb. 13 6 64	t. cwt. lb. 9 10 110	t. cwt. lb. 3 13 14	t. cwt. lb. 61 9 34
Number of raids	9	15	13	6 (a)	18 a)	10 (a)	5	average 13·7
Of the number starting on raids. Percentage of machines which bombed the objective	75	71·5	77·9	67·6	88·2	87·6	87·2	average 79·3
Number of Service Flights	119	229	139	105	201	115	43	951
Number of Practice Flights	66	155	266	532	183	189	16	1407
Total number of Flights	185	384	405	637	384	304	59	2358
Average daily time Service Flying (b)	h. m. 22 11	h. m. 16 40	h. m. 10 4	h. m. 6 48	h. m. 11 54	h. m. 8 0	h. m. 9 34	
Average daily time Practice Flying	6 6	3 24	7 16	14 36	5 1	5 18	1 9	
Total average daily flying time	28 17	20 4	17 20	21 24	16 55	13 18	10 43	
Enemy Aircraft "Destroyed" (c)	—	2	4	1	3	—	2	12
Enemy Aircraft "Out of Control"	1	—	2	—	2	2	—	7
Casualties to Flying Personnel (d)								
Killed	—	3	9	5	12	—	—	29
Wounded	2	2	4	2	7	1	—	18
Prisoners	2	2	11	—	7	—	2	24
Other causes (e)	1	4	8	7	13	2	—	35
Total casualties	5	11	32	14	39	3	2	106

NOTES. (a) In August there was one raid, in which less than 4 machines left the ground, in September 6, and in October 2.
(b) The times given are those actually spent in the air each day.
(c) Vide Note 1. "Explanations of terms and abbreviations."
(d) In computing figures of casualties an individual is counted under one heading only, e.g. if a pilot or observer was taken prisoner, wounded, and afterwards died of wounds, he would be included under the heading "Killed." Deaths or injuries caused by flying accidents are included under heading "Killed" or "Wounded."
This heading includes those lost to the Squadron through sickness, return to England for a rest, or because of inefficiency and transfer to other units.
The Squadron was available for operations for 11 days in May and 10 days in November.

www.ingramcontent.com/pod-product-compliance
Lightning Source LLC
Chambersburg PA
CBHW030401100426
42812CB00028B/2793/J